Winning
Is the Result
of Faithfulness

Dr. Wendell K. Rome's

Winning
Is the Result
of Faithfulness

*A Resource Guide
for Parents to Support Their
Children in Athletics*

ORANGE *frazer* PRESS
Wilmington, Ohio

ISBN 978-1949248-883
Copyright ©2025 Dr. Wendell K. Rome
All Rights Reserved

No part of this publication may be reproduced in any material form (including photocopying or storing in any medium by electronic means and whether or not transiently or incidentally to some other use of this publication) without the written permission of the copyright holder except in accordance with the provisions of Title 17 of the United States Code.

Published for the copyright holder by:
Orange Frazer Press
37½ West Main St.
P.O. Box 214
Wilmington, OH 45177

For price and shipping information, call: 937.382.3196
Or visit: www.orangefrazer.com

Book and cover design:
Orange Frazer Press with Catie South

Library of Congress Control Number: 2024916437

First Printing

Dedication

In the summer of 1979, I went out for the junior varsity basketball team at McDonogh 35 Senior High School. "Thirty-five," as we called it back then, was the only all African-American college preparatory high school in New Orleans. After three months of practicing, in October 1979, I started junior varsity as a small forward. Unfortunately, progress grades came out that October and I had an F in biology. My father, Daniel Rome, had only a few rules, and one was we could only participate in extra curricula activities if we kept our grades up and passed all our classes. My father blew a gasket and told me I had to quit the team. I was devastated but was determined to play on the team anyway. The next day I went to practice but Coach Douglass our basketball coach, pulled me to the side and said, "Rome your father called today and told me you are not allowed to play on the basketball team."

So, I played on a recreational team that 10th grade year to keep my skills up. In 11th grade I did not go out for the basketball team but played every chance I could. My senior year I went out for the team at 35 and made it. Not playing for two years really took a toll on my game, especially my basketball IQ, and so that senior season I only got to play in two games. Riding the bench was the beginning of my understanding of faithfulness. Without that lesson in 10th grade, I do not think I would have learned that playing athletics is a privilege, and academics are a priority. Although I went to church every Sunday with my mother, Dad was not a church going man. Yet he taught me the meaning indirectly of Matthew 25:21 and I am grateful for that life lesson. I would learn in life, that Winning Is the Result of Faithfulness. While other players were getting playing time that season, I was on the bench falling deeper in love with sports and really developing a passion for the privilege of competition.

I dedicate this book to all the athletes, families, and organizations I have served during the last thirty-three years. They have embraced my concept of Winning Is the Result of Faithfulness. This book is a tribute to you all. I express my gratitude and love to you all. Peace, love, unity, and respect to all of you.

Acknowledgments

This book draws from my many years of coaching.

The stories shared throughout the book come from my life and from serving with diverse groups of athletes, colleagues, and parents. In some instances, I have chosen not to use the names of actual participants to protect the confidentiality and privacy of athletes, parents, and the institutions I have served over the years. I first started working with youth in 1989 as a senior at Southern University in New Orleans. It was an internship at Kennedy High School in New Orleans, which sought to support males at risk in the school. That inspiring experience at Kennedy High School led me to work with a program at Incirlik High School, Incirlik AB Turkey in 1991 with their male at-risk program. I coached my first team in the fall of 1991 at Incirlik High School, which was the girls' volleyball team. Dr. Robert Kethcart, the principal at Incirlik High School, asked me to coach the team because we did not have anyone else in the school to coach the girls. Also in 1991, while at Incirlik, Dr. Kethcart allowed me to coach the boys' high school wrestling team. A few years later in 1993, while studying at the University of Northern Iowa, I met Dr. Keith Crew, director of the Graduate Program in Public Policy at Northern Iowa and he introduced me to a teen at risk program which I served in for two years. Dr. Crew and Dr. Kethcart gave me my first opportunities to coach and work with kids and I am very thankful for the opportunity they both gave me.

First, I acknowledge my wonderful wife Kathleen who encouraged me to finish this work I started in 2011. I appreciate her love, support and prayers while completing this project. Secondly, I am indebted to all the athletes, families, and organizations I have served during the last thirty-three years. They have embraced my concept of Winning Is the Result of Faithfulness. This book is a tribute to all of you. I express my gratitude and love to all of you. Peace, love, unity, and respect to you all.

Table of Contents

Introduction xi
1 .... Coaching is a Calling 3
2 .... Learning to Be a Cheerleader! 23
3 .... My Family Is Unique 37
4 .... How to Embrace Lack of Playing Time 55
5 .... How to Stay Involved 65
6 .... Never Focus On Winning or Losing 71
7 .... Parent Code of Conduct 79
8 .... Coaches Code of Conduct 85
9 .... Social Media for Athletes 95
In Closing 107
Endnotes 109
Bibliography 113
About the Author 117
Coach Rome's Coaching Record 119
Twenty-five Parent Tips (A Summary) 121
Sample Practice Plan 12U 125
Sample Practice Plan Junior High Basketball 127
Sample Letters for Parents
to Recruiting College Coaches 129
Coach Rome's Player Evaluation Form 133

Introduction

🪈 Early Years in Kansas City

The vision for this book began with my own experiences of faith, family, and sports. My birth name was Wendell Keith Merritt, and I was born in Kansas City, Kansas, to Pearlie Mae Burks and Luke Jackie Merritt. Early on things did not work out between my parents. I was told mainly because my father Jackie loved women and was a womanizer. In 2002, while pursuing the Doctor of Ministry at United Theological Seminary, I was doing a spiritual autobiography and found out that I have four other siblings by my biological father Jackie. I did reach out to four of those siblings but only one of them, Reeva, wanted to maintain contact. My parents divorced when I was five, and, later my mom met Daniel Rome, my soon-to-be stepfather, but I refer to him as my father. Daniel was a member of the Air Force, and was stationed on a base in Kansas City, Kansas. In 1969, Daniel adopted my brother Dante and me and our last names became Rome. Also, in 1969, after they married, the four of us moved back to Daniel's hometown, in New Orleans, Louisiana.

The fact that Daniel was an only child meant two things. First, that the large, extended family I was used to with my mom went away once we moved to New Orleans. Second, that Daniel, having grown up with no siblings, had a selfish nature. In 1999, after he heard me preach at Austerlitz St. Baptist Church for the only time, he admitted the reason he moved us from Kansas City was he was insecure about my father Jackie and feared he and my mother would get back together. The sermon I preached was, "Have you caught any fish lately?" That sermon encouraged him to tell the truth and it is the only sermon my dad has heard me preach in the twenty-eight years I have been in ministry.

Humble Beginnings in New Orleans

My humble beginnings are significant because they would lay the foundation for my attitude about faith, family, education, and athletics. Once we moved to New Orleans, we met our grandparents and great-grandparents. Meeting these new family members was both good and bad. While I grew to love many of them, I also saw the dark side of human nature. Many boys grow up in silence after having suffered sexual abuse as a child. Child sexual abuse is the exploitation of a minor for the sexual gratification of another person through sexual contact or sexual interaction.[1] My grandfather, Daniel Rome Sr., though a nice man on the surface, was a pedophile and on two occasions propositioned me for sex. The first time was traumatic. Grandpa asked me, "If I would give him some booty, he would give me a few dollars." I said, "No way." He then said if I told anyone he would kill me. I lived in fear during that time, and I was only eight years old. It was by the grace of God that I never gave in to him. I knew it was terribly wrong. I never said anything to my parents about my grandfather's sexual perversions because my grandfather said he would kill me if I said anything. I was also afraid of being further isolated from my new family since my grandmother was saying very hurtful things to me like, "Your sister is so much smarter than you. You will never be anything in life."

Sports in Elementary School

I tried my hand at baseball, basketball and even football one year when I was nine. Athletics was my outlet where I was accepted, made friends,

Comiskey Playground, mid-city New Orleans. Athletics provided an outlet for me.

had good coaches and built healthy relationships with other children. It also kept me away from our home at times when my parents were not around since we lived on Palmyra St. in a double shotgun house right next door to my grandmother, grandfather, great-grandmother, and great-grandfather.

Grandpa Mason, my great-grandfather, was a tremendous man who was in his seventies when we met. I felt safe around him and he took the time to teach me many things including what it meant to be a Christian. This did not come through his words but by his behavior because Grandpa Mason was a man of few words. Grandpa Mason was the head deacon at Austerlitz St. Baptist Church where we attended service. My grandfather was not a Christian and never attended church. He spent his weekends in the clubs and juke joints in uptown New Orleans. Grandpa Mason baptized my brother Dante and me when we were eight and ten years old. I spent a lot of time with Grandpa Mason in the summers before he died. When I was in fifth grade coming home from school, I found out Grandpa Mason had had a stroke. He did come home but later died and that was devastating for me because he was so good to me and our family. Grandpa Mason embraced the fact that I chose to pursue athletics and gave me this scripture to live by as an athlete:

1 Corinthians 9:24 "Know ye not that they which run all, but one receiveth the prize? So run that ye may obtain."

I would compete my hardest on every team and always try to be a good witness while believing being faithful would lead me to success and winning. Grandpa Mason taught me how to keep my faith while being an athlete.

In the third grade, I attended the elementary school of Frank T. Howard No. 1. One day in the school yard I was playing a game, running through, and sliding on the pavement and broke my right arm in three places. I wore a full cast for most of third grade and learned to write with my left hand to do schoolwork. The broken arm prevented me from playing sports that year but not the following year. So I tried my hand at contact football. I began to play at Comiskey Playground between Tulane Ave, Banks, and Canal St. This was a tough place to begin playing sports in New Orleans because at the time all the players were African American and all the teams we played against were African Americans as well. I struggled to find playing time and learned early that football was not my sport. I had a terrible coach, Leroy Johnson, if you were not a stud, he did not have any time for you. This is where a parent watching out for their young athlete would have come in handy. Things like extra practice or throwing the football with them could be extremely helpful. Most importantly being present at practice and even games, being a cheerleader for the team and your athlete.

After that season I never played football again and instead began to play basketball and baseball. I spent so much time at Comiskey Playground that my parents had to put restrictions on the days and times I could spend there. We did not have good basketball courts or a good baseball field, but I did not care because I loved both sports so much. The basketball court was of course outdoors and concrete. At age eleven, I became exceptionally good at baseball playing first base, so good, in fact the coaches moved me up to the Babe Ruth team to play some games with older boys.

Sports in Middle School

I graduated from elementary school and attended middle school from grades 6-8 at Samuel J. Peters. Peters was a tough school located at Tulane Ave. and Broad St. right across from Parish Prison, the local parish jail. This New Orleans public school opened in 1913 and was originally named after Samuel J. Peters, one of the founders of the city's education system.

In the early 1990s, it was christened Israel Meyer Augustine Middle School, after the first African American elected as a judge in Louisiana's Criminal District Court. Today, Peters is empty which is a shame given its rich history in New Orleans. When I attended Peters from sixth to eighth grade it was a remarkably diverse school that had residents from the mid-city neighborhood but had many students from areas like the Iberville project that was in the downtown area off Canal and Orleans St. One of my boyhood friends, Robert Norris, aka Ironhead, was from the Iberville project. We got to be best friends and after my mother accepted it, I began to spend nights in the Iberville projects with Ironhead and he spent some nights with my family where we lived on Palmyra and later in New Orleans East. Peters had racial challenges and tension between African American and Latino students that seemed to never end. We had a school lock down during my sixth-grade year because the racial tension and fighting was so severe. With the tension at school and home I decided to take on something new and play an instrument in the band. My father got me a tenor saxophone which I hated. Quite frankly my heart was in sports, and I turned to middle school basketball to fill the void in my life.

I excelled academically and was on the honor roll every quarter at Peters and I was in a bilingual program. I became a standout basketball player and built a good relationship with my coach, James Ford. He was one of my favorite coaches and I loved him because he was fair and gave everyone a chance to play. One Saturday we had a tournament, and several players were hurt. I had played the entire game for our third straight game and was exhausted. We were in the championships, and I somehow stole a pass and got turned around and made a layup at the wrong basket. That was one of my most embarrassing moments as an athlete, but Coach Ford knew I was exhausted and made it okay.

When I was in seventh grade we moved to New Orleans East to a genuinely delightful home, but I did not see it as a blessing. Dante and I refused to go to the neighborhood schools which had predominately white students. So, I continued to attend Peters and rode the RTA for an hour one way five days a week. Dante attended McMain High School, a magnet school in uptown New Orleans and had an even further bus ride on the RTA than me. My sister Danielle was the only one of us who attended a private school. She attended St. Anthony of Padua from first through eighth grade and then attended Ursuline Academy, an all-girls school in uptown New Orleans.

It always troubled me that my father came to very few of my games and never knew how talented an athlete I had become playing baseball and basketball. The exception would be one baseball season in New Orleans East at DiBenedetto playground in the tough 12/13-year-old league when my father coached the team with Coach Alvin Stokes.

I graduated from eighth grade and was assessed to go to high school at the very prominent and historic McDonogh 35 Senior High School. I was one of a handful of students from Peters to get accepted into 35. To my disappointment, living in the suburbs of New Orleans East at 5001 Coronado Dr. was not a blessing to me at the time. We

DiBenedetto playground in New Orleans East.

were the first African-American family on the block and in 1975 that was not a good thing. I had to walk three blocks to get home after I got off the Broad/Chef Menteur Highway RTA, and every day I was in fear of being called nigger, being spit at, or having rocks thrown at me by the white boys who attended Abramson High School in New Orleans East.

One day I thought, "This is it. I cannot take it anymore." I told my mom how afraid I was, but all she could say was, "The Lord will protect you." In my mind I thought, *"Is that all she can suggest?"* But that was it and the Lord did protect me because even though I continued to experience being called a nigger, being spit at and having rocks thrown at me and other things, I was never attacked by any of those white boys. One time however, when I was in eleventh grade a white man tried to run over me and two of my friends while we were riding bikes against the traffic. He hit my bicycle, destroyed it, and injured my foot badly which is why I walk with a limp today. The worst part of the day was that my father slapped my mother in the face. I called my dad to tell him what happened, and he drove to where I was. My mother later pulled up and he yelled at her, "I told you to let me manage it." He then reached for her car and slapped her in the face. I grabbed him and said, "This is the last time you are going to hit my mother." That was the third time I witnessed my father physically attack my mother. The other two times I was younger, and they were a lot more brutal with my mother bleeding and badly hurt both times. To my knowledge that was the last time he ever put hands on my mom.

🗝 Sports in High School

Looking back on those years I do not believe that my parents knew how to support me as an athlete and how to instill what winning is all about. Ironically, my father, was a strict military man and disciplinarian, who did instill in me what it means to tell the truth, be committed and faithful even though these are characteristics he clearly struggled with. My parents lacked the tools to be supportive of me in athletics and though it was something they encouraged it was not something they promoted or invested in fully, especially financially. For example, in tenth grade I wore sneakers from Sears called Winners. They were not leather shoes and not particularly good for basketball. At a scrimmage against Brother Martin High School, Coach Doug looked down at my shoes and said, "Rome, you are going to need to get some better basketball shoes son." The other players on the team ridiculed me because I had cheap shoes that were not appropriate for basketball. I did not care and that did not stop me from working hard and excelling on the court. Though we were by no means poor, living in a four-bedroom home in the suburbs of New Orleans East, I did not dare come home and ask my father to purchase additional shoes. The answer, I knew, would be no.

 I did not play basketball at McDonogh 35 my freshman year because my parents thought I was too young at fourteen to stay late at school for practice. Instead, my freshman year I played at Joe Brown Gymnasium New Orleans East on Read Blvd.

Joe Brown gymnasium in New Orleans East.

Joe Brown was different from Comiskey where I grew up in the city. For example, this was a gymnasium and not an outdoor concrete basketball court. Our team was exceptionally good and did not lose a game in the city league. I was always the leading scorer on the team and our opponents figured out early that they needed to stop me. All starting five players on that team went on to play high school basketball at different schools in the city. At Joe Brown, Coach Terry was a good man and a good coach, and I loved him. He was a young dynamic, innovative coach who knew how to integrate all his players in the game plan. That's where I learned that basketball is a game of strategy. Coach Terry believed in my basketball skills and really trusted me as a player. After freshman year I was ready for high school basketball.

During the summer heading into my sophomore year, I went out for the basketball team at 35 and was doing well. Coach Doug was the varsity coach and Coach Hicks was the junior varsity coach. We practiced hard twice a day in July and August before the school year began. Our team was like the makeup of our school: all the players were African American and from every area of New Orleans. Coach Doug and Coach Hicks were also African Americans. I was extremely comfortable on the team since I grew up in downtown New Orleans before moving to the suburbs. A few weeks before the season started, we had an issue in practice where varsity players had been skipping running their laps. Coach Hicks was the one who noticed. When Coach Doug found out, he said, "Joe point those niggers out." One by one varsity players began to be cursed out and were asked to leave the gym, and just like that their basketball career was over at McDonogh 35. There was a lesson here. Coach Doug was trying to teach us that players must be faithful in practice. I took a valuable coaching principle from this that I still apply to my players. How you practice is how you play in the game. There is no magic wand or magic formula for winning. In other words, Winning Is the Result of Faithfulness and it starts with being a good citizen and choosing to do what is right for no other reason than it is the right thing to do. That day in practice we ran fifty laps and Coach Doug blew a gasket but that did not happen again where players cheated on laps, warm-ups, or anything. But while basketball was going well for me, academics were a problem for the first time. It was time for progress grades, and I knew in a few classes such as biology and french that I was not doing so well.

McDonogh 35 was the only African-American college preparatory public high school in the city of New Orleans. At 35 we played athletics in district 10 4A which consisted of several high schools such as John McDonogh, Clark, Fortier, Booker T Washington, Landry, and Carver. What all the schools had in common they all had a student enrollment that consisted of all African Americans. However, McDonogh 35 College Preparatory School did not tolerate poor academic performance. I got my progress grades and had an F in biology and knew my father was going to have a fit. The rule in our home was that you had to get good grades and stay out of trouble to play sports. I was so afraid that day to bring my grades to my father because I knew he was a man of his word when it came to discipline. After Dad read the grade report, he told me my basketball days this season were done. I cried and was heartbroken and pleaded for more time to bring my grade up. My mother and brother pleaded with my father also, but he would not hear of it.

This would prove to be my second cornerstone to Winning Is the Result of Faithfulness, that an athlete must keep up their academic grades to be eligible, either by the school or by their parents. I was determined to play anyway and thought I could bring my grade up, so I went to practice the next day anyway. I agree with my father's decision, just not how he applied the rule in our home. Turns out the issue of academics and athletics is not a new issue. In a piece published by Time.com, UCLA professor Daniel Oppenheimer theorizes that many student-athletes fail due to an impulse to fit into a culture where the perception is that academic performance is unimportant.[2] My father in his wisdom had called Coach Doug and told him not to let me play. Coach Doug called me to the side that day in practice and said "Rome, I am sorry, but your father called and said you are out. He told me you would be here today but asked that I not let you practice." I was crushed because I was the starting forward on the junior varsity. I had gone to practice twice a day all summer coming from the suburbs of New Orleans about an hour ride on the RTA one way. And just like that I was out and that devastated me.

Without basketball, I was lost at fifteen years old, and my grades did not get much better. I did bring the F up to a B but resented my father for months and I don't think our relationship was ever the same after that. I ended up going to summer school that year at Warren Easton for English and algebra thanks to my mother's support. I began to shoplift, however, just to spite my parents. Once with three friends and their mother, I shoplifted at a Kmart and got caught by the store security and the New Orleans police were called. They took me to juvenile lock up and I was more afraid of my father than the police. I called Mom right away, but she refused to get me. Her words rang out and they were words many children hate to hear, "I am going to let your father manage it." About four hours later, Dad showed up and when we talked in the car he said, "Wendell, you have been through a lot tonight and I can tell you fear what is next. I am not going to do anything to you because I know you have learned your lesson." I never stole anything ever again. I also stopped hanging out with those boys. I did not rat the other two boys, Peter and George, out to their mother or the police. I learned a valuable lesson about choosing your friends which is something my mother would always preach about. One of my friends George, who I spent time with graduated high school and robbed a McDonald's. He went to jail for a few years and was raped while there.

1 Corinthians 15:33 "Do not be misled: "Bad company corrupts good character." *NIV*

At this point in the spring of my sophomore year, I did not have basketball and baseball season had not started yet. I went to a dance at St. Mary's Catholic all girls high school and got jumped by some boys from Abramson High School. A month or so later I took a family friend to a dance and when walking her home, right off Orleans St. and Broad in mid-city New Orleans I was held up with a gun in my face. I remember passing one man sitting on some steps on a dark street. He whistled up ahead and the man flipped around and put the gun in my face. All I had on me was a gold chain, a pair of sunglasses and seven dollars and they took that from me. I recall one of the robbers saying, "Man I ought to bus a cap in your ass for wasting our time." Things continued to spiral as I began drinking and smoking weed. At my lowest point I turned back to my faith to help ease the pain from my childhood and what had been a safe haven in sports that had been taken away from me. I decided to get a job to gain some independence at fifteen.

Even though I was only fifteen, I got a work permit and was hired at Jim Dandy Fried Chicken. The crew at Jim Dandy really nurtured me and loved me as I was the youngest worker there. My parents only allowed me to work a few hours during the week, Friday, and Saturday.

Sunday in the Rome house was reserved for church and during football season the New Orleans Saints. We went to church every Sunday aside from my father who only attended church a few times that I can recall during my upbringing.

Mom was the church secretary for over thirty years until she moved to Dayton, Ohio, in 2005, after Hurricane Katrina. My junior year I had lost my thirst and passion for athletics and became active in school clubs. I began to hang out with Dr. Leonard Lewis III A.K.A Duggie who would become my best friend and together we started a social club called CHIPS. We were the first social club at the school and had parties. I did not go back to the basketball team until my senior year at the encouragement of my friends who mostly were basketball players including Duggie, Bird (Thomas Keelen) and Black (Melvin Jackson). Two seasons of not playing school basketball took a toll on my game and I had lost my edge. I worked hard and made the team but could not crack the top eight players and spent most of my senior year on the bench. Coach Doug was still the coach and we got along well but I do not think he ever forgot what happened my sophomore year. He did hold that against me and asked me one day, "Rome is your dad going pull you again?"

Our tenure in the suburbs of New Orleans East would last from my seventh to twelfth grade years in high school. Despite the challenges of living in the neighborhood on Coronado Dr. they were some of my best years growing up in our family. All I recall is a little explanation that we were moving from our home in the suburbs back to the city in a two-bedroom apartment three blocks from my high school on Esplanade Ave not too far from Claiborne Ave. It turns out, we lost our homes and cars to bankruptcy, and my parents were soon divorced. My senior year was filled with turmoil, and I was too embarrassed to tell my friends we had lost everything. I just knew at this point basketball shoes were not something my father would pay additional money for. My first pair of leather basketball shoes, Nikes, I bought for myself after working at Jim Dandy Fried Chicken.

I did not understand Coach Doug's concerns back then but after years of coaching I now understand dealing with unruly parents. In our YMCA 10U tournament the summer 2022, I had a player, our point guard, who did not show up for the game. His parents did not call or text that he was not going to be there. One of the main ingredients between player and coach is trust, and Coach Doug never trusted that I would make it through the season. Unfortunately, he was right. Frustrated by my lack of playing time and what I felt was poor coaching, I left the team before the final three games of the season. I was not faithful in finishing what I started. I regret that decision and ever since have not quit anything else I have committed to, which has been another great lesson. Fortunately, the poor coaching I received that season and sitting on the bench allowed me to learn more about the game because I spent so much time watching and analyzing it.

With everything going on in my basketball career my mother was a source of constant support. It would have been nice if my father had sat down with Coach Doug and myself and together, we could have discussed and planned for me coming back to the team. I think that commitment and support from my father would have made the difference in how Coach Doug would have managed me as a player and person. However, through it all I learned, the third cornerstone in Winning Is the Result of Faithfulness, that an athlete must be faithful in developing their skill set no matter what the circumstances. I did graduate from high school and all four of my best friends Duggie, Bird, E-man and Black were headed off to college. The summer after graduation in May 1981, I was blessed to work for Duggie's father, Ruben Robertson at Atlas Coleman American Moving company in New Orleans. Mr. Rub was a wonderful man and further taught me how to be faithful. He had a rule in the morning that if I got to their home around 7am I could ride with him to work and if not, I had to catch the RTA. Most mornings I made it on time, but I came to learn that Mr. Rub was a man of his word, and I deeply appreciated the lessons of faithfulness from him before he passed away. I am blessed to

February 9, 2024, Mardi Gras Zulu Ball. Left to right Eric, Wendell, Leonard, and Thomas.

have the same group of male friends from high school. Forty-seven years later the four of us have remained close except for Black who is deceased.

Sports in the Military

I joined the Air Force in July of 1981 and it was my father's idea. I disagreed with my father's decision to join the Air Force. I was going to join on the buddy system with my friend E-man (Eric Thomas) who later decided not to join and so did I. Later that day I came home and told my dad and he was furious. Dad never cussed much but he told me "Wendell, who gave you permission to start making f___ing decisions? I am the only one in this house that makes decisions." So, dad called the recruiter right away. He told the recruiter I was going to sign up the next day, which is exactly what I did. I left for basic training on October 14, 1981, with a love for basketball and a desire to get in college. I made the best of my air force career. I arrived at Reese Air Force Base in Lubbock, Texas, in December 1981 in the middle of intramural basketball season.

Reese was a pilot training base and home of the T-37 and T-38 aircraft. I was a firefighter so that meant I would be on the civil engineering squadron team. Our basketball team was incredibly good every year I was at that base and the guys embraced me as a new player. I was the seventh man in the rotation and earned more playing time as a small forward as the season went on. I developed a nose for the ball and was the leading rebounder in the league. With my friend Paul Fillman, a 6'6" swing man and a firefighter, we won the championship my first year. Every year after that we won but our team was different the following years in 1983 and 1984. Our lineup changed to Tim as the leading scorer at shooting guard with Keith at point guard and me at the small forward. This line up would get us two more championships and we became a running team.

My son Wendell was born on March 5, 1984, in Dallas, Texas. The spring of 1985 I left active duty and went back home to New Orleans to attend Delgado Community College. At Delgado, I met a wonderful man, George Hansberry, who would not only become my mentor but a father figure until he passed away. I became very close to Mr. Hansberry, and he guided me through life while in my twenties and encouraged me to be faithful in my studies at Delgado and later Southern University at New Orleans.

I later transferred my military duty to Keesler Air Force Base Mississippi, home of the C-130 aircraft. My best friend Duggie asked me to join his basketball team in the New Orleans City league and I agreed. It was an incredibly good team and the four seasons I played on we went deep into the city playoffs each season. I was the sixth man all seasons and started some games depending on who showed up. I was also a college student full-time and worked full-time as a security officer at Barton Protective Services and kept myself in great shape.

By the time 1990 came, I was married to my first wife, Darla, and after graduating from Southern University at New Orleans, I left New Orleans and joined Darla at Incirlik AB Turkey. I had met Darla in 1983 while stationed at Reese Air Force Base in Lubbock, Texas. Darla was a nurse on active-duty.

I began collaborating with athletes of all levels of society while in Turkey and once we got settled, I met Don and Jan. Don was a hooper who was on active duty, so we played basketball every Saturday morning at the base gym. The Gulf War happened and in April 1991 the base began to settle down and we had tent city on base with many individuals from all over the world and all branches of the military. We played a lot of basketball. My son Keaton was born in February 1991, and I continued to play a lot of basketball. I was also an Air Force Reservist serving on the base as a Fire Department Quality Assurance Evaluator and worked at the high school as a learning-disabled specialist.

I joined the administrative squadron basketball team, and we were also exceptionally good. My two years in Turkey, our teams won the base championships, and we really dominated the league with a fierce running game. One game we played a pilot squadron, and it was the toughest team I had played in a long time. I was guarding this guy and he was a huge man. I could not get around him in a half court set and only scored eight points in that game. We lost that game by six points and for the first time I was outplayed. I asked one of my teammates, "Who is that big guy I was guarding?" My teammate laughed and said "Wendell, that is Chad Hennings from the Air Force Academy. He is the eleventh round NFL draft pick of the Dallas Cowboys." Chad was the 290 overall pick in the 1988 draft. I laughed and thought okay now I do not feel so bad. I shook hands with Chad and we both said, "Good game, man." And wished each other the best. Hennings went on to graduate from the United States Air Force Academy in 1988 and eventually earned his A-10 fighter pilot wings by 1990. From 1991–1992, Hennings was deployed with the 92d Tactical Fighter Squadron and flew forty-five missions to help aid in relief and humanitarian efforts in northern Iraq. Following his promotion to captain in 1992, Hennings decided to retire and pursue his football career while he still could and joined the Dallas Cowboys roster—the team drafted him in 1988 even though he was set to fulfill his military commitment.

After Turkey I had a six-month tour of duty at Bitburg AB Germany. I moved to Cedar Falls, Iowa, in January 1993 and met Ron Bigelow a wonderful man and was awarded a full scholarship to study Public Policy at the University of Northern Iowa. Ron was a great friend and mentor and we stayed in touch until he passed in February of 2019. Ron would send me an email every morning to encourage me. His favorite saying was "the only difference between a good day and bad day is our attitude." I often remember those words from Ron when I am having a challenging day. For my faithfulness at Northern Iowa as a student and student ambassador, I was selected to present the student graduation address at the fall 1994 commencement. My sister Danielle received her master's degree in English also. We were the first sibling pair to receive their master's degrees at the same time. The winters were harsh in Iowa, but I made the most of my free time and began to enjoy other areas of sports such as WWE wrestling, motorcross, bull riding, arena football, tractor pulls, the Globetrotters and my favorite Monster trucks. I still enjoy Monster trucks and at-

November 6, 2022, Monster Truck Jam, Dayton, Ohio.

tend the shows quite often. Grave Digger has always been my favorite Monster truck.

One fall weekday during the 1993 Northern Iowa football season I was in the UNI-DOME locker room after playing basketball and met Kurt Warner then star quarterback for Northern Iowa. I would see the football players in their training room across from the men's locker room and sauna. One day I was in the sauna and Kurt came in with a few other players. Everyone said hello and I said, "Great game Saturday, Kurt." He said, "Thanks, you were there?" "Yes, and you all are doing an excellent job." Warner did not start until his senior year and was named Gateway Conference Player of the Year. Warner graduated in 1993 and his story is well known but when I realized he was in the NFL, I remembered meeting him and still appreciate today how he remains humble with all his success. Warner went on to play professional football in the NFL for the St. Louis Rams, New York Giants and Arizona Cardinals.

Warner joined the NFL Network in 2010 as an analyst following his 12-year NFL career. He is in the Pro Football Hall of Fame, is a two-time NFL MVP, and Super Bowl XXXIV MVP. He models Winning Is the Result of Faithfulness and shares his faith openly through many vehicles such as athletics.

In 1994, I met Bishop Paul V Beets, senior Pastor of Gospel Tabernacle Church in Cedar Rapids, Iowa. After being at the church for a while, I became a Deacon. I studied and was mentored by Bishop Beets for two years and in 1996, the Lord Jesus Christ called me into ministry to preach the gospel. I was still in the military and started seminary that year as well. This was a drastic switch and life changing experience because I was on my way to law school after being the first African American to graduate with a master's in public policy from the University of Northern Iowa. I asked Bishop Beets what my requirements for ordination at the church would be. I must admit that his reply really shocked me, and it took me years to not only understand what he meant but how to appreciate what he told me. He said, "Wendell, I am going to examine your faithfulness." I neither agreed with nor understood his criteria, so I asked for clarification. Bishop Beets said, "Are you paying your tithes, coming to church, living as a good witness, learning all you can as a new minister and serving with a loving obedient attitude?" Bishop Beets taught me an unbelievably valuable lesson in that for one to be successful he must be faithful. Bishop Beets introduced the terminology of faithfulness to me which I would apply in all areas of my life including coaching. I am eternally grateful to him for not only being my father in the ministry but teaching me a valued principle in the life of a minister and coach.

In 1995, I married my second wife Alesia, who I met at the University of Northern Iowa in the spring of 1993. Initially, when I accepted my call to ministry, Bishop Beets did not want me to attend seminary. Bishop Beets said, "Why would you want to waste your talents on those inmates." I felt a strong call on my life to pursue ministry as a chaplain which strongly went against protocol in African-American churches. The fall 1996, I enrolled in Dubuque Theological Seminary in Iowa and needed a ministry placement, so I chose the Lynn County Correctional Facility in Cedar Falls, Iowa. Here is where I met Dr. William Jamison a retired correctional clergy. Dr. Jamison would become my field placement advisor as a student chaplain although he was emeritus at Dubuque. I served the men in the Lynn County Correctional Facility for six months. I met with Dr. Jamison weekly during this time. After Dr. Jamison heard me preach my first sermon, he told me, "Wendell, your preaching lacks authenticity. It is boring right now but do not lose heart." He said, "Develop your own style. Just be faithful and God will give you your own style of preaching." Dr. Jamison encouraged me to be who I am and be comfortable with developing my style of ministry which has served me for a long time. I would also take Dr. Jamison's encouragement into my coaching career which I attribute to so much of my success.

We later moved to Iowa City, and I transferred to the Iowa Air National Guard as a Fire Protection Specialist as an overage. I quickly cross trained as a Safety NCO on base. I served for four years as the Safety NCO in the Iowa Air National Guard. I would later cross-train into my third job in the Air Force as a chaplain. These transitions were not easy but as I continued to be faithful, my knowledge and skill set continued to grow while reinventing myself. Athletics is that way, too, in that players must be willing to grow and develop if they are blessed to continue playing extensively, and not be afraid to reinvent themselves. This is what the great NFL quarterback Tom Brady did when he left the New England Patriots and joined the Tampa Bay Buccaneers eventually winning another Super Bowl with Tampa. Brady did not let fear or change hold him back from going on a new journey.

After serving as a deacon in our church, I felt a strong call on my life and in 1996 became a chaplain candidate as a second lieutenant in the Air Force Reserve. In 1997 we moved to Dayton, Ohio, and I was in the Air Force Reserve at Wright Patterson Air Force Base. I was also now in Seminary at United Theological Seminary pursuing a Master

December 1994, Safety NCO School at Lackland Air Force Base, Texas, (SSGT Rome back row third from right).

of Divinity and working at Airborne Express as a safety coordinator in aircraft maintenance. Chaplain Wilton Blake, Chief Chaplain at the Dayton Veterans Administration, was one of the first people I met in Dayton. Chaplain Blake gave me my start in the Department of Veterans Administration Chaplaincy. During those years I worked on Saturday and Sunday as a student chaplain while attending seminary. One day I asked Chaplain Blake, who was only on duty on weekdays, "How will you know what I am doing on Saturday and Sunday if you are not on duty?" He replied, "Wendell, I will know if you are being faithful because the staff around the medical center will inform me if you are not doing your job." This made me think of the reggae song I used to love, "Action Speaks Louder Than Words." Chaplain Blake would never check on me the thirteen years I worked for him at the Dayton Veterans Administration hospital, but he taught me further that being faithful was essential in serving. When Chaplain Blake retired, he appointed me as the youngest chaplain on staff and with the least experience. When Chaplain Blake made his recommendation to the assistant director he stated, "Wendell has learned how to be faithful, that is why I am selecting him to fill in as chief chaplain." I have learned this concept of faithfulness in my military career and have chosen to pass it on to my athletes with remarkable success. I served as Chief Chaplain from 2010 to 2022 when I retired from the Dayton Veterans Administration.

Although my knees began to bother me, I continued to play basketball. In 2002, I played my last season of organized basketball at the Xenia YMCA Christian City League. That year we made it all the way to the league championship and lost by ten points to a much younger and more athletic team.

My basketball career was over, but I had been coaching for years at this point. I would begin working with athletes more aggressively and developed:

The Cornerstones for "Winning Is the Result of Faithfulness."

1. An athlete should be a good witness including citizenship and sportsmanship while learning how to win and lose with a positive attitude. An athlete should do the right thing always for no other reason than it is the right thing to do.
2. An athlete should be faithful with their academics.
3. An athlete should be faithful in developing their skill set and take ownership of their own growth and development. An athlete should embrace a contract with themselves.

Arrested for Alleged Domestic Violence

On November 10, 2014, I experienced a life changing event. I was arrested on an alleged domestic violence charge. After going to court several times, the charges were dropped and the case was dismissed in July 2015. I had a wonderful criminal defense attorney who did an excellent job representing me in the case, James Ambrose.

The news report said, "A domestic violence charge against the chief chaplain of the Dayton VA Medical Center has been dismissed, according to Montgomery County Municipal Court records. Wendell K. Rome, 51, had faced the first-degree misdemeanor charge after he was accused last November of shoving a relative at a Trotwood home, causing the alleged victim to fall and injure her elbow and strike her head on a cabinet, according to a police report."[3] The ironic thing was we had a disagreement about whether Destiny, our daughter, should play basketball as a seventh grader after never having played basketball at Dayton Christian or the local YMCA. I wanted Destiny to play at the YMCA to gain some experience and knowledge of the game. Against my suggestion, her mother took her to practice at Dayton Christian. The other thing about this was

Mugshot from November 10, 2014, Montgomery County, Ohio, jail.

Alesia and I had an agreement in our home that she would manage the children's academics and I would manage the sports aspect of their lives. Alesia violated a long-standing agreement in our marriage and made a sports decision.

A week after the arrest, Alesia filed for divorce. Patricia Campbell was my family court attorney throughout all the proceedings. Patricia represented me from 2014 to 2022 and did an outstanding job. To this day, Alesia and I have not had a conversation about why she filed and wanted a divorce. The divorce was final in June of 2016. It was a bitter divorce that lasted in court from November 2014 to June 2016. At the heart of the divorce were three issues: the house, child support and spousal support. There was no debt and no other issues to resolve. During the divorce, Alesia changed attorneys seven times which continued to delay court proceedings. She also requested a change in magistrates three times which further delayed our case. What really hurt was each time she changed attorneys I was not able to get parenting time with Destiny because her attorneys always asked for continuances so they could get caught up on the case.

The last time I had parenting time with Destiny was May 2015. I was never able to attend any of Destiny's basketball games or other sporting events due to Alesia continuing to fight me in court. Destiny graduated in May 2020 and is now in college. We did settle on child and spousal support, and I also allowed Alesia and Destiny to stay in the house until Destiny graduated high school. We finally sold the house on October 31, 2022. Child support ended September 2020 when Destiny turned eighteen and spousal support ended in July 2022 which totaled nearly $3,000.00 per month for seven years. To my disappointment, I do not know where Destiny resides today, and she has chosen not to have any contact with me. I spent about $90,000.00 on attorney fees in family court trying to gain parenting time with Destiny with no success. My coaching career was on pause for four years while I sought to heal because the story of my arrest was on all local news outlets and on social media. In the fall of 2014, I had just coached the girls' soccer team at Dayton Christian Middle School and I began to coach the freshman basketball team in November 2014. After the arrest, Dayton Christian decided to terminate my coaching contract since they had seen the story on Channel 7 news.

Military Retirement

In May of 2016, through all the turmoil in my personal life, I was finally able to retire from the Air Force after thirty-five years of service with dignity and honor even after all that had happened the last two years. It sadly included my former wife calling my unit commander Col. William Dehaes complaining about our custody case and telling him about the domestic violence case, too.

After retiring from the Air Force, I sought help for PTSD and other physical challenges and finally took the time I needed to heal. The PTSD came from serving in both Desert Storm 1991 and Operation Iraqi Freedom 2007. In Operation Iraqi Freedom, I was the senior hospital chaplain at the Joint Base Balad Hospital where I witnessed the horrors of war for all branches of the military, host nationals and local Iraqi citizens including enemy prisoners of war. I was not prepared for the number of children I cared for who were patients at the hospital who had been injured in their villages. From 2007 until I sought treatment in 2016, I experienced nightmares, waking up in cold sweats and fearing crowds. I was put on several medications including Zoloft, zolpidem, and prazosin. I went through the Department of Veterans Affairs PTSD program in Cincinnati and had a counselor at Kettering Medical

Counseling Center. I have been seeing a therapist all these years and highly recommend counseling for anyone dealing with the challenges of life that are heavy at times. I continue receiving care for my physical and mental health challenges from the Dayton Veterans Administration and encourage all veterans to please get the care you deserve to enjoy your life and not suffer in silence.

Remarriage and coaching again

It was a long journey, but I was determined to gain some mental stability after my military service and divorce. I feared that I would never find love again. But on October 31, 2018, I remarried my friend of over twenty years, Kathleen. Through the marriage I was blessed with the three children she already had: Ronnie, Rya, and Lauren. I also have a wonderful father-in-law, Jim, and mother-in-law, Barbara. I coached Lauren's co-ed youth team at Northmont SAY soccer. I felt very rusty after not coaching for a few years, and it felt like starting all over again with very young athletes. But we had a great season making it to the third round of the tournament. Lauren gave me a run for my money, getting to know her and trying to be her coach at the same time. She was estranged from her biological father and expressed a desire to spend time with him and so we would pray together about it. She finally did get to spend some time with him although it was short lived. When Kathy and I got married, Lauren decided to call me Dad and let her father know she meant no disrespect but felt comfortable calling me Dad. Today, I have a very loving relationship with Ronnie, Rya, and Lauren. Our family continued to grow, and my niece Namandje moved to Ohio from St. Louis, in 2018. Her son Gregory also moved here, and we developed a wonderful relationship. Gregory wanted to play soccer and so I volunteered to coach his four- to six-year-old team at Northmont SAY Soccer in the fall of 2019. I had not coached kids that young before. I remember one practice, a player

6U SAY soccer league and tournament second place finishers. Gregory is the fifth player from the right, 2019.

who was four asked me to change his pull-up diaper. I thought, "Man I did not sign up for this." Our team started 0–2 before we ran off ten straight victories, won three games in the tournament and lost in the tournament final in a shootout to the team that beat us in our first game of the season. I learned that the concept Winning Is the Result of Faithfulness is not dependent on age groups during this season. The formula works at all age levels.

I later followed Gregory to the local Kleptz YMCA in Englewood, Ohio, where he wanted to try his hand at basketball. I coached through all the fears of COVID-19.

Gregory moved back to St. Louis, and I decided to stay with the team of four- to six-year-olds. Despite the inevitable learning curve of coaching young kids verses high school students, the concept of faithfulness is still working. On March 13, 2020, President Trump declared COVID-19 a national emergency. We had been preparing for this all season at the YMCAs here in Montgomery County, Ohio. We made it through that basketball season, and everyone stayed healthy. Some parents decided not to allow their athletes to play but most of our athletes trusted the process

Kleptz YMCA 6U basketball team (start of COVID-19), 2020.

of the YMCA and me as a coach to keep their athletes safe and healthy. We not only played basketball but thrived as a sports community during the pandemic.

Coaching during the COVID-19 pandemic

I did not coach the summer of 2020 due to my studies at the University of Dayton Law School. Most of the parents I talked to were not going to let their children play out of fear and concern. Most parents did not want their young athletes vaccinated which I totally understood. Serving as a chaplain at the Dayton Veterans Administration I had received the initial vaccination and later the booster. In April 2020, I volunteered to deploy to the Detroit Veterans Administration to assist on the COVID-19 ward as a staff chaplain. Detroit was designated one of the hot spots. The experience in Detroit during the pandemic was very rewarding as I was able to serve veterans and non-veterans who were sometimes terminal with COVID-19.

Kleptz 8U YMCA winter basketball, 2021.

When the winter 2021 season came, the YMCA was ready with good protocols in place. Some parents still did not trust allowing their athletes to play. I was happy to coach but our winter 2021 team struggled and only won half our games. Many games we barely had enough players to put five on the court. In the end we all learned that faithfulness is critical in times of natural disaster. We made it through the season with masks on during practice and the games and no one got sick.

I hope my thoughts and reflections in this book will help parents, coaches, and athletes understand and embrace the formula for winning not just in athletics but life.

Parent Tip 1

Do not use academics as a tool for discipline. Instead set academic goals that are realistic for your athlete. Teach them the value of education so they will first take as much pride in their education as they do with their sport. You may track their grades online and more importantly have weekly meetings if the athlete is struggling in a particular course. If necessary, speak to the classroom teacher, coach, and school counselor. Formulate a plan between all concerned people. You might call it a contract or covenant. Take the player off the team as a last resort.

Matthew 25:21 "His lord said unto him, well done, thou good and faithful servant: thou has been faithful over a few things, I will make thee ruler over many things: enter thou into the joy of thy lord."

Three Cornerstones for "Winning Is the Result of Faithfulness."

1. An Athlete should be a good witness including citizenship and sportsmanship while learning how to win and lose with a positive attitude. An athlete should do the right thing always for no other reason than it is the right thing to do.
2. An athlete should be faithful with their academics.
3. An athlete should be faithful in developing their skill set and take ownership of their own growth and development. An athlete should embrace a contract with themselves.

Pro-tip From Coach Rome

Faithfulness is the sole measure of winning.

Determination + Dedication = Faithfulness in Athletics

Winning
Is the Result of Faithfulness

1 Coaching is a Calling

Kleptz 8U winter basketball team league champions. The Elite 8 of the 64 team regional tournament, 2022.

🔔 The Call to Coach

Former National Football League coach Tony Dungy said, "It's about the journey mine and yours and the lives we can touch, the legacy we can leave, and the world we can change, the world we can change for the better."[4]

There have been several college and professional athletic coaches such as John Wooden, Jim Valvano, Tony Dungy, Lovie Smith, Joe Gibbs, Frank Reich, Dean Smith, Hubert Davis, Monty Williams, Mike Krzyzewski, and Dawn Staley who have not shied away from publicly acknowledging their faith as a part of their coaching career.

Hubert Davis claims that while he played for Dean Smith at the University of North Carolina, Coach Smith encouraged him and other players to go to church every Sunday. One Sunday in the fall 2009, I was flying home to Dayton, Ohio, from Air National Guard duty in Des Moines, Iowa. In uniform at the Chicago O'Hare airport, I looked up and it was basketball legend Coach Tubby Smith. He walked up to me and shook my hand. We talked casually as people around us took pictures and it was an honor to meet him. He told me his brother served in the military and that he really had a heart for veterans. I asked Coach Smith if he could give me one piece of advice what it would be. He said, "always watch what comes out of your mouth and try to control your tongue." He noticed the cross on my uniform and said, "thank you Chaplain for your service." I have tried to remember those words of encouragement from Coach Smith and other coaches I have met through the years. These coaches inspire other coaches on the path that coaching is a calling.

When Covid-19 ended, many players, parents and coaches were skeptical about coming back to the YMCA with all the buzz in the media about the vaccinations. We did have a talented team that winter of 2022 and I began to recruit coaches since there was such a shortage. I began to ask potential coaches questions to see where their heart was. "So, you want to be a coach of a youth sport. My question is what is your reason for getting into coaching? Is it to get involved with athletes? Is it to be your child's coach? Were you thrust into coaching because the organization your child plays for does not have enough coaches and you were recruited?" No matter what the reason, God has given you a platform and message to share with your athletes. I really like how Pastor Rick Warren puts it in his book, *The Purpose Driven Life*. Rick says our Life Message has four parts to it:

- *Your testimony:* the story of how you began a relationship with Jesus.
- *Your life lessons:* the most important lessons God has taught you.

- *Your godly passions:* the issues God shaped you to care about most.
- *The Good News:* the message of salvation.

Even for non-Christians, Rick's point about spreading the good news in athletics can still apply to your life. No matter Christian or non-Christian the message of being faithful still applies in athletics and winning. Whatever your reason for getting into coaching, it is essential that you understand that "coaching is a calling." When joining the Dayton Christian coaching staff, I told Tony Pitts in my interview that I believed coaching to be a calling. One day when I was talking to Ken Laake, the athletic director and head basketball coach at the Miami Valley School in Dayton, Ohio, in 2011, I told him coaching was a calling. I also told him that for me coaching was a part of my ministry. I joined the coaching staff at the Kleptz YMCA in Englewood, Ohio, in 2019 and told Darrin Roth the same things. After all these years I still believe these statements which I believe continue to allow me to coach with such love and passion. I do not do it for the wins or losses, but for my offering to God. A sports coach is a person who provides instruction and guidance to athletes on how to improve their performance in a particular sport.[5]

🐚 The Coaching Journey Began

In my senior year at McDonogh 35 Senior High School, there was an open basketball tournament with students who were not basketball players. I coached a team of boys that won the tournament, and everyone was surprised my team did so well and were not the favorites to win. As a seventeen-year-old coach I taught my players what it meant to be faithful and that if every player could follow their assignments, we had a good chance of winning. I saw coaching as a calling from an early age and knew deep inside one day I would pursue that calling.

Ironically, the players, most of them underclassmen I did not know but built a chemistry with, bought into my philosophy quickly and we won. In addition, we were the only team who used prayer as a tool for unity, peace, comfort, and confidence.

Mark 11:24 "Therefore, I say unto you, what things soever ye desire, when ye pray, believe that ye receive them, and ye shall have them." *NIV*

What happened to me playing basketball at McDonogh 35 drove me to be a better coach than what I had at 35. It forced something inside me to say that every athlete needs a coach that will believe in their God given talent and be willing to help develop that talent. I was not only frustrated by my lack of playing time but the fact that my father just did not see fit to invest in my development as an athlete or young man, given how much I loved basketball and how hard I worked to get better. Like many couples, my parents were going through their own issues and ended up divorcing when I graduated and left to go to the Air Force. I remember during my eleventh-grade year my father telling me, "Wendell, me and your mother will be getting a divorce because I just do not want to be married anymore." A few years later he would marry again and start another family. I do not think my father ever really knew how good a basketball player or athlete I really developed into.

Coaching Basketball

After several seasons in baseball, I began volunteering at Dayton Christian helping with third and fourth grade basketball intramural games. Although I began coaching sports in 1991 in Turkey, I started my official basketball coaching career in 2005 as the high school boys' basketball coach at Dayton Christian School in Dayton, Ohio. The year

Dayton Christian 7th grade Metro Buckeye Conference Champions, 2004–2005.

before 2004, I was the middle school boys coach, and we won the Metro Buckeye League Conference. In August 2005, I was fresh back from being MIA during Hurricane Katrina after going to New Orleans to be with Duggie after his mom, Ms. Thelma Robertson had passed away. We did not get to have the service due to Katrina. My experience during Hurricane Katrina drove me to want to be the best coach at the high school level. During one of our first games, we played a freshman team at Beavercreek High School. We were in trouble from the start as it was our first game of the season.

Coach Tony Pitts who was, at the time, the varsity boys head coach and athletic director for Dayton Christian asked me, "Coach Rome is that really the score?" I hate to see a kid get hurt like this no matter what, but when you try to showboat while you are up by forty points nothing good comes from that lack of sportsmanship. Later in the fourth quarter they were shooting threes, and one player went up and attempted a dunk. He lost his balance and crashed to the floor on his right arm. The young man was yelling and screaming in pain as he rolled all over the floor. This was the first-time coaching in all my years that I felt humiliated and embarrassed because of the score. The referees cleared the players off the floor, and we all stood watching as the athletic trainers tried to care for the young man. I went over and kneeled and told him, "Son I am a chaplain; can I pray for you?" He yelled, "Yes please, please, please, please, please." I bent down next to him and held his hand and laid my other hand on his arm. This was while hundreds of people, fans, and players were watching. He finally calmed down and then the ambulance took him to the hospital. While leaving he cried quietly and told me, "Coach, I do not know how to thank you."

We finished out the game with the last two minutes left and still lost by forty points. Later that night I received a phone call from a parent who knew this athlete's family. She told me that the young man had been struggling with girls, alcohol, obedience, drugs, grades etc. He told his mother that night at home that he was going to change his ways and become a more faithful athlete. Even though we lost the game by a blowout, in the end we still won as a team and program. I won that day as a coach and learned a continued lesson on coaching being a calling.

Philippians 3:4-8 "Yea doubtless, and I count all things but loss for the excellency of the knowledge of Christ Jesus my Lord: for whom I have suffered the loss of all things, and do count them but dung, that I may win Christ." *NIV*

I learned early on that coaching is about more than wins and losses and it is not about me. Coaching is about developing and bringing out the God given talent in each player that I have been entrusted with at that time. Of course, the forty-point loss to Beavercreek was not my only struggle as a life-long coach.

My first coaching championship in basketball came at Dayton Christian Middle School with the eighth grade team in Dayton, Ohio. The first championship was in the 2004–2005 season in the Metro Buckeye Conference. A great conference and we had players like 6' 10"

Adreian Payne at Jefferson High School who would go on to star at Michigan State and was the fifteenth pick in the 2014 NBA first round of the Atlanta Hawks. God rest his soul. Payne was killed on May 9, 2022, in Orlando, Florida.

Our teams at Dayton Christian competed against Payne for several years. I remember sitting in the gym before my freshman games and talking to him. He was always polite, respectful and a joy to be around. He was a beast on the court, and I honor our time together and the fond memories I have of him. The overall record of this team was 17–3, which would feature Aaron Deister, Ohio All State point guard at Dayton Christian as a senior in 2009. This group of athletes would go on later in their senior season at Dayton Christian to be in the final four of the State of Ohio boys' basketball championship in 2008–2009. I have used the same philosophies on each team coached and been blessed with players buying into my philosophy. I was hired in the fall of 2005, by the new athletic director at Dayton Christian, Tony Pitts to coach the freshman boys' basketball team and was also a varsity assistant coach. Coach Pitts joined Dayton Christian as the athletic director and head boys' basketball coach. We had a great relationship, and I began talking about winning from a perspective of faithfulness with him. Coach Pitts taught me the value of having a practice plan, scouting teams, tracking statistics in practice and games, how to prepare for teams through game film and research.

In 2006–2007 as the freshman boys coach at Dayton Christian we went 16–3 and lost by two points to Jefferson High School in the championship game after having a twenty-three point lead at halftime. One of my most painful losses as we allowed Jefferson to outwork us during the second half as we got complacent and stopped being faithful and got beat. That freshman year at Dayton Christian I had a point guard who was upset that he did not make the junior varsity. His attitude was sour the first week and also after we announced the teams. We brought him in and told him he had to decide if he

Dayton Christian 9th grade basketball team Metro Buckeye Conference Champions, 2006–2007.

would continue in the Dayton Christian program because his attitude would not be tolerated. I had another meeting between myself, the parents and athlete and explained to him why he needed more time on the freshman team to develop his skills. I am not sure how much of a difference it made because the athlete transferred to another school his sophomore year believing he would get more playing time at a local high school in Springboro. I am not sure what became of this athlete, but I heard he did not get much playing time at Springboro by the time he was a senior.

The summer of 2006, we had our basketball camp at Cedarville University. Cedarville hosted a wonderful camp where high school players from Kentucky, Ohio, Indiana, Michigan, and West Virginia played basketball games for one week. We typically had three or four basketball games in one day. This was a wonderful time and allowed me to get to know my freshman players before the season started. This was where I met head Cedarville basketball coach Ray Slagle.

Slagle took over a Yellow Jacket basketball program and in eight years built it into one of the best in NAIA Division II. His program was 177–92 overall and 92–46 in the American Mideast Conference. That was the result even after laboring through an initial campaign of 8–22 and 3–15 AMC in 2000–01. Coach Slagle's resume is most impressive but what I learned from him further taught me the meaning of Winning Is the Result of Faithfulness. On a Tuesday morning, the week of the summer tournament, an older gentleman said his wallet was stolen. Coach Slagle got all one thousand basketball players in the gym and said the following. "This gentleman has had his wallet stolen. I expect within the hour that his wallet will be returned. When you return the wallet, you will be prosecuted. God has placed a mechanism inside all of us called a conscious. I expect whoever stole this man's wallet to return it immediately. Gentlemen we are here to play basketball and be Godly young men." Coach Slagle then led us in prayer and within the next thirty minutes the wallet was returned. I continued having success at Dayton Christian as the freshman coach. My second basketball championship was in the season of 2007–2008 at Dayton Christian and we did well even though we only had eight players on the team. We went 19–2 and won the freshman league.

I later had success at Miami Valley School coaching the middle school team for two years, the freshman team for one year, and finally, in 2013, coaching the junior varsity. I was coaching the freshman team at Dayton Christian in November 2014 when I got arrested for domestic violence against my second wife Alesia. With all the chaos in my private life, I took four years off from coaching and was not sure I would coach again. I started counseling with Dr. Peach at Kettering Counseling Center in November 2014, went into the PTSD program in the Cincinnati VA in August 2016 and started seeing Dr. Miller at the Dayton VA who is still my therapist today. I coached my first co-ed team at the Kleptz YMCA in December 2019 and began my ninth season at Kleptz June 11, 2024. I have coached the U6, U8, U10, U12 and junior high

Kleptz winter YMCA 10U regional basketball championship trophy celebration, 2024.

teams. Six of my nine seasons we have won the local league, our tournament and went on to play in the metro YMCA league. Many of my athletes now play for their perspective schools which I think is so cool.

I tell my basketball players not to look at the scoreboard at halftime. I want them to not focus on the score, so we spend our time asking one question, are we being faithful with the game plan we put forward despite the score? I look at each player's skill set initially but seeing what God can do in that player through nurturing and training. I try to invision not what our team looks like on the first day of practice but what we can be if we are faithful and commit to being our absolute best. This means we do not play for ourselves, but we play for each other and most importantly represent our faith.

Coaching Baseball

Coaching baseball in Trotwood, Ohio, in 1999 at Butcher Field was very tough but we did have some success. Being new to the area I did not know any of the athletes except my son Kevin and my neighbor Devin across the street. Kevin and Devin would be my two pitchers for several years. I went to the first draft, and I recalled guys laughing at me because of the team I selected. I even selected one female who I later would become remarkably close with and today she is a police officer here in Ohio. That year, as I stated elsewhere in the book, we got throttled many times. One day Dustin our catcher said, "Coach Rome, I noticed we keep doing all this praying and we are not winning at all." Dustin was deeply troubled because losing is hard, and it can eat away at your spirit. We were getting better but moral victories do not always mean a lot in sports. I noticed a change in Dustin's attitude as we began to do better. I saw Dustin in Kmart five years later and he thanked me for what he learned while playing baseball for me. He was studying welding in high school.

Our baseball team was young, inexperienced and we played like it most of time making mistakes that would cost us big run innings. In other words, we would play well to a certain point and our pitching would break down, a player would miss an easy ground ball, or we would get thrown out on the bases at critical times. Well, we kept praying and being faithful and the next season we were the best team in the 9/10-year-old league. Prayer was the glue that held this team together during the good and tough times. Prayer is what gave me and the players hope that we would get better, and we were not defined by how many games we won or lost but rather if we were faithful. What defined this team at the end of the day is that they learned how to be faithful through hard work and dedication. Dustin did not play that season with us because he was too old but saw us play a lot and told me he was grateful things were working out and he was being faithful to his new team.

In 2001, I coached a 9/10-year-old baseball team in Trotwood, Ohio, that went 1–20. We got better as the season went on, but we were the laughing stock in the league. Teams would run up the score on us like 25–2.

Summer 2001, Butcher Field
F-minor baseball team.

I think the thing that really hurt was at the end of the season no parents came up or even called to say thank you. It made me realize that for many parents it is about winning, and parents do not always appreciate the pain in developing a championship team. In other words, parents can be very fair whether they love you when you are winning and do not talk to you when your team is struggling. I had to travel for military duty that next season at the baseball draft. I had a plan early in the season to teach and look to next season as I had many players who had not played baseball before. I asked Alesia if she would be willing to go and draft the same twelve players from the previous season. She said, "Wendell you are crazy, you do not mean that you are going to take the same players, I mean the team was terrible." I said here is the list, please follow it to a tee and draft these players and they will be available because no other coaches will want them because they do not know how much better the players have gotten. She reluctantly agreed and selected the same twelve players. That season we lost two regular season games, won the league, won the tournament and I was named manager of the year in 2002 and 2003.

More importantly, the parents joined in and agreed to work with their athletes on days that we did not have practice on basic skill sets that I had developed for each player. This is an exceptionally good example of how when the parents, coaches, and athletes are on the same page it can be a beautiful thing for the good of the team. I discovered that it was not important to talk about winning and losing but how to be faithful in all aspects of the game. During the 2004 season it was exceedingly difficult to keep preaching this philosophy, but it is one that I have committed to and believe in 100%. If an athlete can be taught how to be faithful, then winning will be the blessing and outcome of that faithfulness. I must admit that my teams may have been short on talent but not on being faithful with our assignments once players bought into the philosophy. We commit to outworking the other teams in all aspects of the game. A parent asked me once, "Coach, how do you get away with playing all those players and winning, we just do not see how you do it." I told him I just do it and my players expect to play because we discuss playing time very openly and when substitutions will be made. Every player knows that they will be expected to enter the game early and contribute. It is

Summer 2002, Butcher Field F-minor baseball team conference and tournament champions.

a formula that seeks to get every player to buy into what their role is on the team. It is a formula that develops trust between player, coach and parent and key ingredients to success. Also, every team needs team players and a player like Dennis Rodman who embraces and excels at their role on the team. Rodman led the league in rebounds per game for seven straight seasons (1991–92 to 1997–98), finishing with an astounding total of 11,954 in 14 seasons in the NBA. Rodman was not only a stellar rebounder but developed into an outstanding defensive player. What I found most impressive about him was being okay with being faithful with his role whether it was with the Detroit Pistons, Chicago Bulls, or San Antonio Spurs.

The key to my success in coaching sports is trusting God and seeing the talent deep inside each player. Two of my favorite scriptures:

Romans 8:28 "And we know that God causes all things to work together for our good to those who love God, to those who are called according to his purpose." *NIV*

Luke 16:10 "Whoever can be trusted with very little can also be trusted with much, and whoever is dishonest with very little will also be dishonest with much." *NIV*

Coaching Wrestling

Earlier I stated in 1991, I coached a varsity boys wrestling team at Incirlik High School, at Incirlik Air Base in Turkey. I had never wrestled or coached wrestling and knew little about the sport but had two great assistants. I did have a long history of watching professional wrestling on television and going to matches in New Orleans, Louisiana, and Lubbock, Texas, my first military duty station. I took the coaching job at the request of the high school principal, Dr. Robert Kethcart, who

Incirlik, Turkey, high school wrestling team
ASTL champions, 1991.

knew how much I loved athletics and working with athletes. Most of my team was made up of players that liked rock and roll and heavy metal music. I do not think there were any Christians on the team that year. I introduced prayer into our locker room before matches. We lost our first match by three points to Izmir High School. We won the second match by twenty-one points and the third match by twenty-four points. We hosted the third tournament at our school, and I got terribly busy setting up the gym for the matches. I somehow forgot to pray with the team before the match and Patrick one of the team captains reminded me, "Coach you forgot to pray for us."

I could not believe how the team embraced prayer and came to rely on it as a source of peace, comfort, and hope. We did pray before that match and won which made us the champions of the 1991–1992 school year in Turkey. This was my first coaching championship developing the theme Winning Is the Result of Faithfulness. The most amazing thing was we were in a Muslim country and had a few Muslim athletes on the wrestling team. I would start off the prayer by thanking the Lord for each player and their abilities. We would always close with:

Matthew 6:9-13 "Our Father which art in heaven, hallowed be thy name. Thy Kingdom come. Thy will be done in earth, as it is in Heaven. Give us this day our daily bread. And forgive us our debts, as we forgive our debtors. And lead us not into temptation but deliver us from evil: For thine is the kingdom, and the power, and the glory, forever. Amen." *KJV*

I started off the wrestling season having to learn the sport but what I did know was how to teach athletes the fundamentals of winning and being faithful. Being a chaplain has taught me something about prayer in that there are situations where it can be a unifying tool such as sports and war despite one's religious affiliation.

🏐 Coaching Girls Volleyball

In fall 1991, I also coached the varsity girls' volleyball team while at Incirlik High School in Adana, Turkey. It was my only season coaching

Incirlik, Turkey, high school volleyball team, 1991.

volleyball and our team was not particularly good, but we had a lot of fun. It was here that I learned the joy of coaching girls and have been working with girls ever since in different sports. My philosophies in coaching have not changed much over the years but my approach to dealing with the players is consistent with our changing generations and cultures.

Coaching Soccer

I coached boys SAY soccer in Trotwood from 1997–2002. We had some good teams through the years and our players went on to play high school soccer and a few even played in college. Before every soccer game I would join hands with the players, coaches and parents and we would pray. Funny, that the two other coaches were not comfortable with that, but I asked them to trust me and let the Lord work things out. During this stretch we won several league championships and two seasons we went to the regional finals in Cincinnati. After one game, the Trotwood

11U Trotwood SAY soccer team, 2012.

league commissioner came up to me and said, "Coach you got a minute? I noticed that you pray quite a bit with your team. How do you get away with that? Any complaints from parents?" I told him, "Commissioner, I just do it! Before every season I give the parents a biography of myself and my coaching philosophy. I informed the parents that I was a chaplain and prayer would be a part of team play and our identity. I knew many of the parents were not Christians, but I hoped they could appreciate the power of prayer in athletics or in life." From 2009–2013, I coached my daughter Destiny's SAY soccer all-girls teams at Trotwood SAY soccer. Our teams were good each year, winning several league championships. The fall of 2014, I coached Destiny's middle school girls' soccer team at Dayton Christian. Before and after each game we had prayer and devotional time.

Remember, Coaching is a Calling

Some of you may currently be a sports coach and enjoy it. Some of you may be coaching sports at some level and trying to decide if it is really for you. I mean between practice, games, managing the players and parents along with your own personal lives can be a bit much. Some may be asking what is the bottom line for me am I making a difference? Have I been faithful in coaching these athletes? Patrick M. Morley in his book *The Man in the Mirror* offers a diagnostic to help answer the question, Have I Been Faithful?

1. Am I trying to win the rat race?
2. Do I fully understand how God keeps score?
3. Am I leading a life of faith, love, obedience, and service?
4. What is my highest hope?
5. How did I score on the Game of Tens?
6. Am I pursuing significance or self-gratification?

7. Am I disillusioned with materialism?
8. Has my passive indifference contributed to the decaying state of the nation?
9. Have I been looking for significance in appropriate ways?
10. Am I willing to pay the price if the cost of being a Christian in society goes up?
11. Am I a talker or a doer?
12. Have I been *faithful* with what God has entrusted to me?
13. Do I regularly study God's Word so He can show me the purpose for my life?
14. Am I contributing to God's agenda? Do I even know what God's agenda is?
15. Am I a cultural Christian or a biblical Christian?

This last point is for parents and coaches. I stated earlier on from coach Tony Pitts how to develop a practice plan. It does not matter what sport or age group you are coaching, a practice plan is of excellent value and a mandatory teaching tool. A practice plan maximizes your time with the athletes and ensures as a coach you are preparing and building skills in your athletes.

Parent Tip 2
Parents ask the coach for a mid-term and final player evaluation of your athlete. Each athlete should know what they need to get better at as the season revolves and ends. Parents should know how to support their athletes in getting better.

Parent Tip 3
Parents do encourage the importance of faith in the life of your athlete. Prayer still works. Do not be afraid to activate prayer. Many Americans support prayer during public high school sporting events, compared with roughly a third who approve of professional athletes kneeling during the national anthem, according to a new survey.[6]

Kleptz 10U pregame prayer March 9, 2024.

Philippians 4:6 "Do not be anxious about anything, but in everything by prayer and supplication with thanksgiving let your requests be made known to God." *NIV*

Coach Mike Krzyzewski said he prayed the Holy Rosary before every game and offered it for some intention and for the glory of God.[7]

Coach Dawn Staley after winning the NCAA women's basketball championship on April 7, 2024, in an interview with ESPN's Holly Rowe said "God is so faithful. God is funny like that. He is funny. He rips your heart out and He makes you believe. He makes you believe the unimaginable. Thank you, Jesus, thank you."

Pro-tip From Coach Rome

Every coach should have a theme or purpose they teach their athletes no matter what sport or level they coach. This can be somewhat fluid, but the foundation of your coaching should remain the same.

2 Learning to Be a Cheerleader!

Dayton Christian 9th grade basketball team huddle, 2007–2008.

🔔 Many Coaches and Referees Do Their Jobs in Fear

I am not sure why parents today are so off-the-hook, misbehaving so badly at sporting events when they are supposed to be there supporting their athletes. It is happening at every level and in every sport in 2024. An example back in the day was in 2007–2008, I coached basketball at Dayton Christian High School. During a freshman game, pictured above at Troy Christian High School, there was an incident under the basket with the two big men from both teams. Our center got tangled up with the Troy Christian center. The Troy Christian center took an elbow from our player and his nose began to bleed heavily and the referee called a foul. The referee said the play was clean and incidental and we moved on with the game. The Troy Christian's players mother could not let it go and starting yelling, cussing, swearing and the referee had to stop the game as she got so out of hand. Her husband took her out of the gym finally and we were able to resume playing. Her son began to cry because he was so embarrassed at his mother's behavior. After the game, several Troy Christian parents came up to me and apologized for the woman's behavior. A day or so later I received an email from the Troy Christian Athletic Director apologizing for the parent acting so badly at the game. She was truly a parent who was off the hook and her language was so bad that she had to be escorted out of the gym and I was told she would not be allowed to return to any other games at the school. I thought what a shame because her son was only a freshman.

Do you yell at umpires, referees, coaches, and your child during competition? Have you been talked to about your behavior? Have you ever thought about how your behavior impacts your child psychologically during competition? Do you know what the true skill level of your child is on game day? Are you a parent that tries to coach your athlete on every play from the stands, embarrassing your athlete? I ask all these questions because over the years I have coached some players who are psychological train wrecks due to the extreme behavior of their parents. Yes, there is a psychology to coaching and working with athletes, but some of their issues can be traced right back to their parents. Unfortunately, I have seen no difference in Christian and non-Christian schools or locations. If you answered yes to any of these questions you are an off-the-hook parent. In an article by John Sullivan, he says the biggest problems in youth sports is parents who will not let the game belong to the kids.[8] In 2022, I saw a referee of a YMCA 8U tournament game so afraid after being threatened by coaches and parents that he literally quit on the spot and refused to referee his last two remaining games of the day. The fans were upset over a few questionable calls in the game.

In the 2011–2012 basketball season, I was the freshman head basketball coach and junior varsity and varsity assistant coach at the Miami Valley School in Dayton. All three of the teams that year had particularly good seasons, but it was the most trying season with parents as they were confronting our coaching staff, were confronting referees and even another coach of one of our teams. During our last regular season game against Yellow Springs High School, a parent had on a shirt that read "Our Coach Sucks." This was a fan of Yellow Springs in our gym at Miami Valley. Head boys' basketball coach Ken Laake said, "Man we thought we had it bad this year." I am not certain of the fan's intention in wearing the shirt, but he stood most of the game until one of our school officials went over and asked him to leave for poor sportsmanship. The sad thing is that the coach for Yellow Springs was a great coach. They were just having a down year. I wonder if the fan thought anything about the example he was setting for his son, who was a player on the Yellow Springs team. The fan was eventually escorted out of the gym because he continued to yell profanity at the Yellow Springs coach, heckling the coach also.

Football Team Chaplain Dayton Christian High School

I was the football team chaplain at Dayton Christian High School from 2005–2009. My experience with football was extremely limited to my one year playing incredibly early in life, watching/attending NFL games and my son Kevin playing since seventh grade all the way to one year of college football at the division 1AA level. When I decided to join the team as the chaplain, I did not know quite what to expect in my role. I would pray for the players and coaches on both teams. If a player made a big play, I would provide pastoral care through a hug, sharing words of encouragement and celebration. If a player made a mistake, I would provide pastoral care as well, offering words of encouragement to uplift the player. During my six years as team chaplain, I began to discover that football and sports were very emotional and mental. In football, if a player fumbles, for example, that one play can change the dynamics of the game. With thousands of fans in the stands when a player makes a mistake like a fumble or turnover, he knows that play could potentially change the game. Quite often when a player does good or bad, their first reaction is to look in the stands for their parents to see what their reaction is to the play that just occurred. I also discovered that players do that to be affirmed by their parents. This affirmation needs to come in the form of support as if to say, "it is going to be all right," and, "we are right here with you."

I remember my son Kevin in his tenth-grade season had sprained his MCL in the first quarter of a football game. The first thing he did after getting injured was look for me. I hugged him and told him it would be all right, and I was deeply sorry he was hurt. He was out for four games with that injury. His rehab went very well and in his first game back against Cincinnati Christian he was very rusty, not catching a pass in live action for weeks. Kevin had not dropped a pass in a game at this point in his career. The fourth pass that was thrown to him during that game he dropped also. To this point, Kevin had not dropped a pass in four years of playing football. He ran off the field and I called him over to me to offer some support and pastoral care not as a chaplain but as a father. Kevin cried like a baby and in the chill of October at Cincinnati Christian Academy he had a meltdown. I wiped all the tears off his face mask, hugged him and prayed for him during that game. He did not catch a pass that game, but it was the first time that I had seen Kevin so emotional in a game of any sport. I asked Kevin the next day what he was thinking when he dropped those four passes. He replied, "I let myself, you and my team down by not catching those passes." I told Kevin, "First you did not let me down, second everyone else understands that this was your first game back from injury so stop putting so much pressure on yourself." What happened to Kevin is what happens to many athletes: after making his first mistake he mentally checked out of the game. As the Dayton Christian football team chaplain and parent of a football player I understood my role on the team.

I did not give the coaches advice, criticize the players and especially my son who was on the team. On the side lines when the offense was on the side lines, I would always position myself to be away from Kevin, so I did not interfere or put any additional pressure on him during the games. I fought hard not to say anything to him other than to provide pastoral care when needed. I was there as the football team chaplain and not as a parent or coach. This worked out very well and I maintained good boundaries between myself, the coaches, and parents. Kevin taught me one of the most valuable lessons as the parent of a star athlete. He asked that we not discuss anything about the game the night of the games. I then learned not to discuss game matters until he was ready. Most times that would be Saturday evening or Sunday after church and dinner. If he asked for feedback, it would go something like this. Since Kevin's biological dad was in his life early in our relationship, we agreed that he would call me Wendell. I was fine with that, and it worked well for us all these years. Kevin said, "Wendell did you see that play when I caught the ball over the middle. I wanted to turn it up field but took a bad angle. What do you think about that play?" I would then remember to always give constructive positive feedback. I would say, "Kevin that was a great catch, it was beautiful. Next time do not break your route off." Then I would ask him, "What do you think you could have done differently?" This type of dialogue always allowed us to have positive interactions all the way until Kevin played in college at Valparaiso and later at the University of Dayton.

🐦 Parent's Role as Cheerleader

I do not think parents realize the seeds of doubt and how negative comments can affect the athletes play come game time. For example, at Dayton Christian we would do devotionals with the football players all week. Every season from 2005–2009 we played a tough football schedule. We played and lost to Ft. Loramie every single season. It was obvious that D.C. players had no expectation of winning from the way we played the game. In 2008, I asked one of the players, "Hey, what are you thinking, it just seemed like you gave up?" He said, "Dr. Rome I just do not believe we can beat Ft. Loramie. We

Parent celebrating Kleptz championship, winter 2024.

have lost to them every year of my high school career and my mother told me to not worry about winning the game because after all Ft. Loramie is a better team than D.C. and you all will never beat them." This is an example of a parent thinking they are helping but really hurting that athlete and the team by planting seeds of failure and doubt in her son.

In my thirty-three years of coaching and working with athletes from various places I have found that the behavior of the parents has gotten worse every year. I am not sure why some parents allow their children to play sports when it is not about the athlete. In other words, some

The Miami Valley School 8th grade team, 2010–2011.

parent's behavior is so bad that it makes it exceedingly difficult for the athlete and coach to have any type of positive player coach relationship. During the 2010–2011 basketball season at the Miami Valley School, I had some remarkably interesting parents.

We had an open gym during the month of October and made the team selections in mid-November for the seventh and eighth grade teams. Once the teams were set, I sent out an email stating which team each player was on and that depending on how a few players developed they may be swung up or down on either team. In early December, I decided to change three players because it was best for them and the team based on performance, statistical data, work ethic and attitude. I made the announcement to the team during a team meeting in the locker room.

The two eighth grade players embraced the change and played on both the A and B teams. The sixth-grade player must have gone home and told his parents of the fact that he was moved to the seventh-grade team. During practice, his mother came up to me during a water break and stated she wanted to talk to me. She wanted to have a conversation about her son's playing time during a water break at practice. I had seventeen players waiting for me to rejoin them while this parent expressed her displeasure with how I told her son about being moved to the one team. Meanwhile, every player on the team is watching this exchange, even his older brother. This parent had no regard for the fact that she was holding up practice and wanted to continue her ranting and raving even after I asked her to talk at another time about her concerns.

A few months later, this same player missed the school bus one Saturday morning at 10am on our way to a game leaving from the Miami Valley School and headed to Troy Christian School, about an hour away. I had coached the seventh-grade game and in between games while preparing for the eighth-grade team, this same parent with her husband confronted me about leaving her son at the school. Again, this was in front of the entire team and parents, the scorer's table, and referees are witnessing this mother going off the hook. Now keep in mind I am not the bus driver, and the team was to report at the bus at 10am. We left at 10:07am and headed to our game with no cars in sight in the parking lot. I did not receive a message from the player's parents saying they were running late so the bus driver said we must leave. In all my years of coaching I have never had such a negative exchange with a parent like this where they were so insulting. She even told me that I did not have a clue about coaching, she mentioned my profession as a chaplain. Okay, now the player is watching this exchange take place between his parents and myself. How was I expected to be able to coach this player from this point on after this second interaction with his parents? We did end up having a good relationship and finished out the season on a good note, but this exchange not only impacted him but the rest of the team as well. Could this entire scenario have been handled better by the parents? Was there a better time to bring up their concerns?

This, of course, was not the first time I was confronted by a tricky situation involving parents. In 2005, along with the help of Dorian Davis, we formed Trotwood Amateur Athletic Association, a non-profit Christian sports organization here in Trotwood, Ohio. TIAA was dedicated to teaching youths' baseball and life skills. That year we had 11/12 and 13/14-year-old teams. Both teams were extraordinarily successful but the 11/12 team that Dorian and I coached won their tournament for the F majors. This was a team that we put together off an ad in the *Dayton Daily News* neighborhood section in the newspaper and held open tryouts. Dorian and I had coached together for many years in baseball and really had a good system. I would take the pitchers, catchers, and infield, and Dorian would take the outfield. I would relay the pitching signs to the catcher who then relayed them to the pitcher. On offense, I was the first base coach and Dorian was the third base coach who also called the batting signs. What Dorian and I had was great chemistry from coaching in soccer and baseball where we had already won a few championships together.

That year we had a parent that was off-the-hook. We never saw the parent at practice but during games he would yell out instructions to his son every time he came up to bat. I am not sure if the parent accepted that his son was taking batting signs or running signs on the bases. During our championship game in Brookville, Ohio, we had the momentum going our way with a 5–3 lead in the second inning. His son came up to bat and got a base hit in the outfield. As the first base coach, I instructed the player to take a little bit of a lead but do not steal second base. We had not done any stealing to this point in the third inning because the other team's pitcher had a good move to first base, and he was still relatively fresh. The parent yelled to his son to run, take the base, steal, and the player took off running. He got thrown out at second base and the player ran off the field crying in embarrassment. To compound things, that was the end of the inning and we had to fight to get the momentum back which we did in the fourth inning. To make matters worse the parent would not stop yelling at the player for getting thrown out until Dorian went in the stands and had a word with the parent. After the game, the parent wanted to talk to me about the incident. We had just won the championship, but he was angry that he caused his son to get embarrassed. I tried to avoid him, but he would not let it go and I finally had to tell him if he did not stop stalking me, I would call the police. He left the ballpark in peace, and we never heard from him again.

    My last example of an off-the-hook parent comes from the summer of 2023 at the Kleptz YMCA. I had been working as a sports site supervisor and was asked to referee a soccer game on Saturday morning for our co-ed 7–8-year-old soccer team. One of the team's head coaches was not there and the game was going fine except for a lot of pushing by both teams. It was physical, and I appreciated the physical play but had cautioned both teams to keep their hands off other players and stop pushing so much. In fact, at one point during the third quarter I blew the whistle and got both teams together to talk to them about the rules and to ask them to stop pushing so much even though the games were tight. I continued play and later in the third quarter I heard a fan yell out, "You asshole." I was not sure who the man was talking to, so I kept calling the game. He yelled out, "Hey big guy with the tattoos, I am talking to you. Do your f___ing job and blow your whistle." I said, "Sir please calm down and stop using profanity or I will have to have you escorted from the field." I reminded him the YMCA is a Christian organization. He said, "Man f__k that, you better start blowing your whistle, or it is going to be some real shit out here." I appealed to his mother and father who were with him, and they got him to calm down. I did not want his daughter to see him escorted from the field or have the police called to settle him down. Unfortunately, it seems like not much has changed with negative behavior from parents during sporting events. I do all I can as a coach to encourage positive parental involvement given the nature of our family systems in 2024. For example, every morning on game day I send a pregame text to the parents. Game time, location, goals for the game, reminder for parents to cheer for each player and let me do the coaching. My system of communication has helped but some parents are just chronically late and refuse to communicate. For example, some players do not show up for practice or the game and I have no way of knowing if they will participate in either. It drives me crazy, but I have learned to not let it get the best of me or impact the team negatively.

The Thrill Is Gone in Sports for Your Athlete

Finally, you know you are an off-the-hook parent when your child, who has played and loved a sport for their entire life, decides they do not want to play anymore because your behavior has taken all the joy out of it. This happened in the fall of 2010 when Kevin transferred colleges from Valparaiso University to the University of Dayton. After he struggled with his fall workout, he decided he was done with football. I told Kevin about the business aspect of him playing football and that a large part of his scholarship money was due to him playing football. In the end it did not matter after I laid it all out to him. The spring of 2011, he got a bill from the Bursar's office at the University of Dayton. I did not have the heart to let him be kicked out of college, so I took out a PLUS parent loan for $10,000.00. He then proceeded to get on academic probation after all our hard work. Kevin's mother had taken all the joy out of football for him and his experience in college. She made it not fun and enjoyable for him, forgetting that he had been a football player for the last seven years and that he knew how to conduct himself with the athletics and academics of the game. She put too much pressure on him to excel when he was already excelling.

The second issue was not that Kevin really wanted to quit football but that he was in love. He met another engineering student, and they were seriously dating. The goals and plans we had made for his life were changing and I needed to accept those changes. Your life goals may change and your athletes may want to try a new path that doesn't include being on a team.[9] An athlete may just fall out of love for the sport and realize it's no longer for them.[10] When Kevin came to me and said he did not want to play football anymore after all the years of blood, sweat, and tears I put in with him, my answer was okay. I knew at this point, despite my pleading with him, he had already made up his mind. What proceeded that spring semester was him having to move back home for a while and we enrolled him at Sinclair Community College in Dayton where he decided not to go to classes there either. To this date in 2024, Kevin did not go back to playing football and he did not get his college degree. Kevin is doing well and is incredibly happy with his life in Hawaii. He works in IT, makes jewelry, and does some singing. My advice to parents is to keep the main thing the main thing and let it be about the athlete and not us as parents. That is the lesson I learned and pass it on to all parents who are willing to listen to the harsh reality of what I learned from pushing too hard and being an off the hook parent!

The examples I have included on the next page of how to avoid being an off-the-hook parent come from BelievePHQ.

10 TIPS FOR SPORT PARENTS

TOP 10 TIPS

#1 FOCUS ON THE PROCESS NOT THE RESULT

#2 AVOID PRESSURING A CHILD ABOUT WINNING OR LOSING

#3 HELP YOUR CHILD TO SEPARATE SPORT FAILURE FROM PERSONAL FAILURE

#4 GIVE YOUR CHILD FREEDOM TO PROBLEM SOLVE AND MAKE THEIR OWN DECISIONS

#5 ENCOURAGE, ENCOURAGE, ENCOURAGE

#6 ALLOW YOUR CHILD TO PLAY FOR HIMSELF OR HERSELF

#7 ENCOURAGE YOUR CHILD TO TAKE RESPONSIBILITY FOR THEIR DECISIONS

#8 WATCH WHAT YOU SAY TO YOUR CHILD

#9 RESPECT AND DO NOT INTERFERE WITH THE COACH

#10 DO NOT CONSTANTLY INSTRUCT DURING TRAINING AND GAMES

@BelievePHQ

Parent Tip 4

I will not be an off-the-hook parent and will respect my athlete, the coach and organization they compete with. I will honor the policies and expectations for parents. I will be a cheerleader for my athletes and their team.

Parent Tip 5

I will only impart positive energy to my athlete accepting that it is not about me. Like my great-grandma used to say, "Wendell if you do not have anything good to say, keep your mouth shut." I will only give constructive feedback when asked by my athlete not on gameday but when my athlete is ready to receive the feedback a day or so later.

Parent Tip 6

I will always remember what God has called me to do in the life of my athlete to be an encourager, be positive and supportive of them, their coaching staff, and the organization of participation.

James 1:19 "Everyone should be quick to listen, slow to speak and slow to become angry." *NIV*

Psalms 127:3 "Children are a heritage from the Lord, offspring a reward from him." *NIV*

"Successful parents of athletes behave like thermostats not thermometers." *John Wooden*

3 My Family Is Unique

May 2023, Rome family photo, left to right: Yvonne (Wendell's son's wife), Kathy (Wendell's wife), Wendell, Rya, Lauren. Second row, left to right: Wendell holding Micah, Ronnie, and nephew Anthony.

In August 2001, I began working on my Doctor of Ministry degree at United Theological Seminary. After praying for months on a dissertation topic I decided to deal with the issues of step-families and in particular what name is fitting for stepfathers. My topic "Call Me Patu; An Alternative Name for Stepfathers" was what my dissertation was about. It felt like a natural and particularly critical issue to write about since I grew up with a stepfather and I have now been a stepfather in two different families. In 2001, I had been coaching for a while but noticed that there were many family situations that were present each season on my teams including same sex families, biological families, single parent homes, stepfamilies, adoptions, divorced parents, grandparents, and foster parents raising the athletes. For example, the family system of my summer 2023, U10 team at the Kleptz YMCA is below:

- *Player 1*—single family mother raising son.
- *Player 2*—single family mother raising son.
- *Player 3*—single family mother raising daughter.
- *Player 4*—married family both parents
- *Player 5*—single family mother, father, grandmother raising son.
- *Player 6*—single family grandmother raising grandson (his mother is deceased)
- *Player 7*—single family mother is raising daughter.

I figured out that to be more effective as a coach I needed to understand what was going on with the family and all the many aspects present in the modern day. One way I gain valuable information about my incoming families is to look at the rosters and see what players have the same last name as the parents. I do not make assumptions, but this gives me a heads up about potential family dynamics I might encounter. Here is an example of my family dynamic which includes several family systems parents may deal with in supporting their athletes. I offer my system as a source of encouragement that you are not the only unique family.

Wendell

My first duty station was Lubbock, Texas, and I hated that base. However, while in Texas I continued to play basketball but lived amazingly fast and loose drinking and partying when I was not on shift as a firefighter. As a result, on March 5, 1984, my son Wendell was born out of wedlock. Through a series of events, Wendell's mother Pat decided to marry another man, Leroy. After fighting with Pat to see Wendell for months after I moved from Lubbock to New Orleans, I agreed to allow Leroy to

May 2024, Wendell coaching his son Micah's 4U soccer team Aubrey, Texas, YMCA.

adopt Wendell in 1986 which is why his last name is Quinn. This is one of the decisions I regret most in my life. I was twenty-one at the time, back in New Orleans and a struggling college student. It seemed like the right thing to do but later Leroy was killed in a car accident in 1987 and Pat called and just like that I was back in Wendell's life. Wendell and I had our challenges in his late teens, but I am thankful today we have a beautiful relationship. We never did try and reverse the adoption even after Leroy died tragically. I offered on several occasions to have his name changed again from Quinn to Rome, but we could never settle on that issue, so his last name remains Quinn until this day. So, I gave up my legal rights to Wendell early in his life, but tragedy brought us back together and I was more than willing to accept my role as a father again. I hope this is encouraging to someone who might be in a comparable situation that God can still work out a relationship with your child no matter what the situation is so please do not lose hope.

Wendell was an exceptionally good basketball player throughout his life. I never saw him play one game until October 2010 in a city league in Arlington, Texas. I sat there with so much joy and even though Wendell was twenty-six, this meant so much to both of us that we were finally together in that capacity. This proves that it is never too late to support your children in life and especially athletics. His team won that day, but it was not about the game but the fact that I was finally there to support him. Wendell was so proud as he introduced me to his coaches, teammates and friends who came out to support their team. After the game I dashed off to Dallas Ft. Worth airport and caught a flight back home to Dayton, Ohio. I must say this was one of my most rewarding moments as a father in supporting my children in sports. I was so proud to be a part of Wendell's life that day. Today, Wendell is married to Yvonne, and they have three children. Paris who is in college, Aiden who is in middle school and plays soccer, and baseball, and Micah who is four and is getting introduced to sports.

Keaton (Deceased)

On October 31, 2015, Keaton was killed in a one car accident in Abilene, Texas. I ordered the autopsy and copies of the pictures from the accident scene. This was challenging to view and read but it did bring me some closure. When Wendell and I went to Keaton's services we visited the accident site and it also was helpful to our healing. I married my first wife Darla in 1989. On February 27, 1991, Keaton was born, and he was a Desert Storm baby. I was so excited at the time to have another son and believed this would be so different since I missed so much time with Wendell. When Keaton died in 2015, we were not on the best of terms. I am not sure how we got there but Keaton was angry and

Abilene High School marching band, 2010.

would say things like, "You never did nothing for me." This all started when he was twenty-two and after all the child support, travel, and court proceedings. (The things he was saying to of all people his grandmother and my mother.) Unfortunately, we did not get to totally clear the air before he passed which used to make me incredibly sad. Even in good relationships where the last communications were sweet and loving, "the griever is often left with the things they wish had happened differently, better, or more, and with unrealized hopes, dreams, and expectations for the future."[11] My grief was tremendous, and I would pray to God for peace. Keaton came to me several times in dreams around his birthday. When I was living in West Carrollton, Ohio, early one morning something touch me, and I heard Keaton's voice say, "Daddy I am all right. I love you. Let your spirit be at peace with our relationship and my death." He came to me in a dream two more times and I am now at peace with his death. I am happy about all the time we spent together especially being able to coach him in sports. In 2021, Kathy and I visited the accident site where Keaton was killed. We met the homeowners who own the property by the creek he drove into. The homeowner told us she remembered the night Keaton went into the creek. This took courage but brought further healing and closure for us. Athletics was one of the things that brought a bond between Keaton and I for which I am very thankful.

Keaton was raised for the first seventeen months of his life in Turkey at Incirlik AB where we lived together as a family. I worked during the day as a special education assistant at the high school on base, coached girl's volleyball, wrestling and had a male at risk program. Keaton's mother worked as a nurse on active duty at the base hospital. Keaton had a Turkish nanny, Naje, who cared for him five days a week during the day. In the summer of 1992, we moved to Germany and took an assignment at Bitburg, AB. This proved to be the end of our marriage as I left Germany in the fall 1992 and later went to the University of Northern Iowa where I pursued the master's in public policy. When I left Germany Darla, my wife at the time, and I agreed to try to work on the marriage from a distance but as time progressed, we just could not keep things together and Darla asked me for a divorce. Unfortunately, things did not work out between me and Keaton's mother and we divorced in 1993.

Following the divorce Keaton and his mother were stationed in Del Rio, Texas at Laughlin AFB and Keaton suffered sexual abuse from one of the babysitters' children. To my knowledge the babysitter would allow Keaton and her two sons to take baths together. The older son would play with Keaton's penis and touch him inappropriately as the babysitter allowed the boys to take baths together. We found out about this in 1997 when Keaton came to visit in the summer, and he was trying to touch Kevin in his penis area constantly usually when we were not around. Keaton also had some learning deficiencies as he was in special education from fourth to twelfth grade. When we found out what Keaton had been trying to do to Kevin, we confronted Darla and she finally admitted what happened to Keaton. This was a very rough time for us especially trying to get Keaton help for being sexually abused because Darla did not agree on the right course of counseling for Keaton, and we fought over the case in court. I was successful in getting court mandated counseling for Keaton to help with his behavior, bad dreams and the fact he had been sexually abused. Keaton admitted with the counselor in Wichita Falls, Texas, that he was having dreams about dinosaurs because of the sexual abuse he suffered. The therapist was able to help Keaton and his behavior improved at school and on visits to our home in Ohio.

Keaton was retained in fourth grade, and this put a tremendous strain on the relationship between Darla and me. As a father who lived out of state in 2003, I spent $20,000.00 in child support, attorney fees, travel, and psychologist to try and get Keaton help with his psychological and educational needs. At the end of 2003, I had exhausted all my funds and was also exhausted physically and mentally. I did not see Keaton again until he graduated in June 2010. I did stay connected with every school he attended during this time. I never did find out all the clinical issues Keaton was dealing with because Darla was not willing to share information or allow me to be part of Keaton's healing as his father.

Through all the turmoil, I was able to see Keaton play soccer for one year in Texas. Another year I saw him play football in a pee wee league. Keaton played baseball with us two summers in Ohio which was very cool and rewarding in having both Keaton and Kevin playing on the same baseball team. Keaton adjusted well and fit in with the other players. In high school, Keaton played trombone in the marching band and was quite good. From 1997–2003, I saw Keaton four to five times a year, typically, during Thanksgiving, Christmas, spring break and six weeks during the summers until 2003, when Darla took me back to court for another increase in child support. My child support went up from $403.00 to $675.00. At the court hearing in San Antonio, I begged Darla to allow for the adjusted rate in the summers when I had Keaton. She would not budge, and I told her at that time if the child support went up, I would not be able to see Keaton as much. That did not seem to matter to Darla.

When I was in Iraq in 2008 at Joint Base Balad, I met a nurse from San Antonio. One day after church she asked to talk with me and said "Chaplain Rome, I know your ex-wife, Captain Rome. We work together at Lackland Medical Center. I want you to know she told me on several occasions she regretted taking you back to court and wishes she would not have done that." I said thank you and it was some sort of consolation but did not fill the void of the greed Darla exhibited and the fact she could not put Keaton first knowing how hard I had tried over the years to have visitation time with him.

Kevin

I met my son Kevin in March of 1993 when he was twenty months old in Cedar Falls, Iowa while studying at the University of Northern Iowa. His mother Alesia and I were friends for a few years and got married

Dayton Christian Middle School football team, 2004.

in August 1995. I met Kevin's father the year before in 1994. We went to the gym, played some hoops, had lunch and some drinks. I asked Big Kevin how he felt about me being in Kevin's life as his stepfather? He said "Wendell, I feel good about it, and you have my blessing." I told him I would always love and take care of Kevin like he was my son. I have kept that promise over the years and most people did not know that Kevin was not my biological son other than our last names being different. Many times, over the years, people would meet me and assume that my last name was Washington. Kevin's senior year we met many football coaches as he was being recruited to play college football. They would always say hello Mr. Washington, how are you? These coaches never even took the time to read Kevin's biography because it clearly stated that our last names were different.

The first sport we introduced Kevin to was gymnastics when he was four. Later that year when we lived in Coralville, Iowa, he played soccer and took swimming lessons at the Iowa City YMCA. I coached the four-year-old soccer team with another coach whose name I cannot remember. Kevin went on to continue playing soccer, baseball, basketball and in seventh grade joined the Dayton Christian football team.

I remember in the summer leading into seventh grade he came to Alesia and myself and stated, "I would like to play football." Alesia and I looked at each other and said you cannot be serious because you do not like contact. We asked Kevin what was behind him suddenly wanting to play football because he was a good soccer player. Kevin said firmly, "that soccer is not a manly sport and the boys at school are teasing me since I play soccer, so I want to switch to football." After much debate and discussion, we gave in and decided to allow him to play football.

The problem was that football practice was not at his Dayton Christian Campus in Trotwood, Ohio, but at the campus downtown thirty minutes away. To compound things, I worked an hour away in Wilmington, Ohio, at ABX Air. I would leave work early, drive to his school and then take him back across town to football practice by 3:30.

We thought he would not last in football but after his seventh-grade season he stated he would like to continue playing football in eighth grade and ended up playing in college. This is why I tell parents not to rush their athletes as they may be a late bloomer in a sport and end up being good. Too many parents start players young and then the athlete gets burned out by the time they are in high school.

My relationship with Kevin as his stepfather is incredibly unique because I have known him since he was a baby. Secondly, I coached him in basketball, soccer, and baseball, and was his football team chaplain. We spent many hours together on the court and field. We have won championships together in basketball, soccer, and baseball where Kevin was the number one or two pitcher. We always worked hard to help Kevin with his schoolwork. In eleventh grade, Kevin was diagnosed with attention deficit disorder (ADD). We were able to get Kevin through twelfth grade with no problem but at times he struggled to stay on task. He graduated from Dayton Christian with a 3.10 grade point average and an overall twenty-two on the ACT. This made him an extremely attractive athlete and student to many colleges as he qualified for the Clearinghouse with no problem. Late in his twelfth-grade year as we were trying to prepare him for college, he began taking Adderall. Kevin had a tough time accepting his ADD diagnoses and refused to take the medication. Sadly, this impacted him in college in his courses at Valparaiso and later University of Dayton. It also impacted him on the football field as he tried to learn a much larger playbook. Once Kevin transferred to the University of Dayton, he decided to hang up his cleats. Kevin said, "I just want to be a student for a change." The truth of the matter was Kevin met another engineering student named Anita and he was in love.

During Kevin's senior year of high school in 2008, I was deployed to Iraq for Operation Iraqi Freedom as the senior hospital chaplain. In late September, Alesia sent me an email saying she needed to talk with me, and it would be a difficult conversation. I called a few days later and she began to tell me how Kevin was struggling on and off the field. I noticed in the football film that I received from Kevin's coach Jamie Rice that he did not seem like the same player. He seemed distracted and his catches per game, yards per game and rushes per game all went down. Kevin met a freshman young lady at Dayton Christian, and they began to date in secret. This relationship almost ruined both their lives because they were both about to be expelled from school for violating several rules like having sex. We were able to mediate discipline and Kevin did graduate as noted earlier but this is a notable example of how distractions can derail an athlete's goals if you are not careful. We used the parental guides on Kevin's phone from AT&T and traced them to find out exactly what was going on between him and the young lady. Parents do not be afraid to trust and verify what your athlete might be doing with their free time. Trust your parental intuition when you believe things are not right. Please do not allow distractions to ruin the plans, hopes and dreams you and your athlete have developed over the years.

In October at Dayton Christian, they would have senior night at the last home football game. Alesia thought she should invite Kevin's father to the game since I could not attend. This was incredibly significant because Kevin's father had never seen him play in a football game or any sporting event to this point. At first, I was very reluctant and did not think it was a promising idea. At that point I was only thinking of myself and the fact that I could not be present for Kevin's senior night. We talked some more for a few weeks and after praying about it I said yes but still did not like the idea. The issue was Big Kevin could not afford a hotel when he came to Ohio and Alesia asked if he could stay at the house. That was exceedingly difficult for me being so far away and my wife's ex-husband would not only be at the football game but would be staying in our home. The weekend seemed to go fine but a month or so later Alesia told me that Big Kevin's wife was upset because Big Kevin lied and told her I was at the house, which was not correct. I was still in Iraq. I later found out that Big Kevin was hoping something sexual would happen between him and Alesia. Big Kevin lied to his wife back in New Orleans telling her I was at the house. This is an example of how a special or unique family situation can be a challenge but putting the athlete first is necessary. It was extremely uncomfortable for me but in the end, Kevin felt good about his father seeing him play for the first time. This incident did, however, damage Alesia's and my marriage because I do not think I ever trusted her again after this. Kevin now lives in Hawaii, works in IT, makes jewelry, has made a few rap songs and is an avid fitness stud. We communicate regularly and I am thankful to still have a relationship with him through the divorce with his mother.

Destiny

Destiny was born on September 17, 2002. I still remember that one day when Alesia came to me and said, "I would like to have one more baby." Honestly, it took me a while to accept the idea but when we both agreed we prayed for a girl and got pregnant within a few months. I was thirty-nine and very content with having three children. Destiny was our only child that we had together, which made her unique in our family. Destiny loved the arts and did praise dance with the Vessels of Honor dance group for several years. She had played soccer, basketball, and golf. Destiny was always a great student and graduated with honors, being in the National Honor Society most of her school years.

I had the pleasure of coaching her SAY girls' soccer team from 8-11 years old. Our team was good, and we did not lose a regular season game but once in all those years. In fact, we were always the league champions and the number one seed in the tournament. We lost in the area champi-

Dayton Christian 7th grade basketball team, 2014.

onship game 2-1 one season, but the next year won and went to the state tournament in Cincinnati. I also coached her middle school soccer team at Dayton Christian in the fall of 2014. I have encountered several young ladies from this championship team. They are all young women now and seem to be doing quite well. On February 26, 2024, I was sitting in the sauna at Everybody's Fitness in Clayton, Ohio enjoying my sauna and the door opened and I heard a voice say, "Coach Rome is that you?" I said yes, it was Ajaya, one of the young ladies from my 2011 soccer team. Ajaya said, "Coach Rome do you remember me?" I said yes you were a striker on our team. Ajaya went to tell me how she and other girls went on to play high school and college soccer and the skills and faithfulness they learned from me have carried them into adulthood. We had an enjoyable conversation and then Ajaya said coach I was just talking to one of my co-workers the other day and I told her your favorite saying "this is not a weekend at Uncle Bernie's." I said you played for me, and we laughed and exchanged phone numbers as Ajaya is in school for photography now.

I talk earlier in the book about the domestic violence incident that happened in November 2014. Oddly, enough the dispute between myself and Alesia was over Destiny playing basketball at the YMCA or at Dayton Christian. After the separation in 2014 I did have some parenting time until May 2015, but battled Alesia in court for four years 2015-2018 spending $90,000.00 in attorney fees and emotionally drained I gave up the court battle to have parenting time with Destiny. She graduated from Dayton Christian with honors in May 2020.

Destiny has chosen to this date to not have contact or communicate with me which saddens me very deeply. I continue to pray for reconciliation with her in hopes of one day soon having a loving father daughter relationship like we once had. I have no idea where Destiny is located currently or what she is doing with her life. Parental alienation is something no parent should ever have to experience through divorce. The divorce was a tough time for me, Wendell, Kevin and Destiny but God did give us all beauty for my ashes.

Lauren

On October 31, 2018, I married my friend of twenty years, Kathleen. She had three wonderful children. Our children are Ronnie, who loved playing in the band and played some sports, Rya, who loved singing and praise dancing, and Lauren, who loved soccer and ROTC at Northmont high school where they all graduated. Ronnie and Rya did not play sports for me, but Lauren played SAY soccer for me the fall 2018 in Northmont's co-ed team. Our team did well, and we made it to the third round of the playoffs before losing. Going into Lauren's freshman year in high school we decided to enroll her in ROTC as a punishment for something that happened at the end of eighth grade. We did not think she would grow to love the military environment, but she did. After her freshman year she continued to want to attend a boarding school, so we agreed and enrolled her in the New Mexico Military Institute in Roswell, New Mexico. She came back home to Ohio finishing her junior and senior year continuing ROTC. Lauren just finished her first year in college. She lives on her own and loves it. Lauren is in college full time and works full time.

New Mexico Military Institute, 2021.

Ronnie

Northmont High School marching band, 2018.

When I met Ronnie, I could tell right away he had a love for music. He performed in the marching band at Northmont High School. He was a section leader and did a great job. Ronnie has become interested in finance and investment and is currently working and studying with Primerica to become a licensed financial advisor. Ronnie lives on his own and loves it.

Rya

Rya is very talented and gifted. She sang in the choir in high school, was in a mentoring class for seniors, and was on the praise team at Mount Calvary Baptist Church. Rya is also gifted in design and is a great artist. She has done the artwork and concept of three of my tattoos and they are wonderful. Rya is expecting her first child, and we are very excited about that. Rya lives on her own and loves it.

Northmont High School prom, 2021.

I did not have much time with my new set of children before they all graduated from high school and moved out on their own to live their lives, but I have a great relationship with each one of them. We do not use the term stepfather or stepchildren in our family. I refer to them as my children and they refer to me as their other dad. Out of the turmoil of my divorce in 2016 the Lord blessed me with another opportunity to be a father and I am so grateful for that. Kathy and I are empty nesters for the first time and coming to enjoy our new life together.

Before I conclude this chapter, I would like to give some advice to parents who are coaching or are considering coaching your children and especially blended families. It can be extremely rewarding and a blessing but only if you can establish strict boundaries with your athletes. If you do not have a great relationship outside of sports, it is not a good idea to try and coach your child. I attended a fifth-grade game recently between Northmont and Mad River Middle School. The Northmont team's coach started his son over a player named Timothy who currently plays for me at the Kleptz YMCA. I noticed in team warm-ups the skill set of his son was not equal or better than Timothy. Yet, the coach as he has done all season continued to start his son. My point here is a coach must be realistic about the skill set of their child on the team. A parent relationship should not outweigh the coaching relationship for the good of the team.

That night, Northmont was in a 15-point deficit in the first half and Timothy brought his team back to win by one point with two seconds left in the game. I got up after the game and introduced myself to Timothy's coach and he tried to justify why Timothy was not getting playing time early in the season. This discrepancy in his coaching cost him several games and did impact the morale of the team. I continued to encourage Timothy to hang in there and work on his game and eventually the coach would see his value on the team. His Northmont coach told me, "Timothy was disappointed when the season started because he was not getting the playing time he was used to. Now, I cannot take him off the floor because I see his value to the team." Timothy scored half of the teams' points and led them in rebounds that game. I am glad it turned out positive for Timothy but for so many kids the unpleasant experience leads them to quitting that sport. I am not saying do not coach your kids but please be fair to the other players on the team.

Today, parents that do not know me think I have a child on my team because I coach for the love of the game and continue with my message

Winning Is the Result of Faithfulness. At sixty years old, I feel very energized and enjoy coaching now more than ever. Be very prayerful about whether you should coach your children. Charles Barkley, former NBA great and analyst, put it best on March 23, 2024, during March Madness when he said, "Players in the locker room who practice with the coach's son everyday know the truth about if the coach's son should be playing ahead of other players." I had a terrific experience coaching five of my seven children in various sports and loved every minute of it. Dan Hurley, coach of the men's basketball team at the University of Connecticut is getting that experience coaching with his son, Andrew Hurley, and they seem to be enjoying the experience.

Relaying Mental Health Challenges to the Coaching Staff

In this chapter I have tried to demonstrate how unique family systems can be successful by using myself as a witness and example with the complexity and realism of my three family systems. Today, our family systems are more unique than ever, and parents struggle to try and figure out how to support their athlete when their family system is different and outside of the box. Please do not forget about families with children who have mental or physical challenges. I have had athletes with physical disabilities such as one leg shorter than the other. I have had numerous athletes with mental disabilities such as ADHD, ADD, anxiety etc. How does a family relay these challenges to the coach and organization they become a part of? Be honest and upfront about the challenges your child and family face no matter how severe. Secondly, trust that if you are honest the outcome will be a positive experience for everyone. We are all created in the image of God, including children, no matter what the challenges. I have learned that it does not matter what your family system is as long as you find a way to support your athlete. If you cannot be at every game or event, set a schedule and make the events or games that you can. I can say as a coach that it will make an enormous difference to your athlete knowing that you sacrificed to support them in whatever sport or function they are blessed to be a part of. Remember, this is all about your athlete and not you as a parent. A final word of encouragement to parents in unique family systems please do not let how you discipline children ruin your marriage or outlook on the athlete playing sports.

Dr. Kevin Leman offers these seven secrets of loving discipline from his book *Living in a Step-family Without Getting Stepped On*:

1. Relationships come before the rules. All the secrets of loving discipline must be used gently but firmly to obtain the best results.
2. The whole is more important than the parts.
3. You are a healthy authority over your kids. In other words, you are not too authoritarian or too permissive.
4. Hold children accountable for their actions. Loving discipline does not punish but lets the child pay a reasonable consequence for misbehavior or a poor attitude.
5. Let reality be the teacher. Using reasonable consequences as a tool and not a weapon in the blended family is an art.
6. Use action, not words. A key to loving discipline is to give children responsibilities, but always reserve the right to "pull the rug out."
7. Stick to your guns. This is an all-important principle, particularly when a child is wailing, crying, carrying-on, or telling the stepparent, "You're not my father!"

These are some of the tools I have used as a guide in two blended families over thirty-one years. My four non-biological children have not been an issue with discipline because we had practical tools that worked, and I hope my story will be useful to you as you navigate the issue of discipline in your nuclear or non-nuclear family.

Parent Tip 7
Do not force your athlete to play a sport that they do not want to play.

Parent Tip 8
Do be realistic about what your athlete's gifts and talents are.

Parent Tip 9
Do involve other family members, parents, if possible, to support the athlete. Divorced families can work together.

Parent Tip 10
If your athlete has a disability such as ADD, ADHD or any other medical diagnosis, do get together with the coaching staff immediately and let them know what the athlete is dealing with so adjustments can be made for the player. Please do not be ashamed of any challenges the athlete may have whether physical or mental.

Parent Tip 11
Do not be afraid to discuss your unique family system with the coaching staff, administration etc. If you are a divorced family and the father or mother will be visiting, calling, or attending the game of the athlete, let the coach know.

James 1:2-4 "Consider it all joy, my brethren, when you encounter various trails, knowing that the testing of your faith produces endurance. And let endurance have its perfect result, so that you may be perfect and complete, lacking in nothing." *NIV*

Pro-tip From Coach Rome
Remember you are a blended family united by choice, woven together by love and strengthened by each other to support your athletes.

4 How to Embrace Lack of Playing Time

Dayton Christian 9th grade Metro Buckeye Conference Champs, 2007-2008.

🏀 Attacking the Coach or Referees Will Not Help

In the fall of 2005, when I was hired on at Dayton Christian as the freshman team head coach and varsity assistant, coaching with Tony Pitts and Kevin Green, we had the pleasure of meeting two of the Holliday brother athletes. James was a senior on the varsity and JT was a sophomore on the junior varsity. Two years later I would have the pleasure of coaching their younger brothers on the freshman team, Paul and Phillip twins pictured above, numbers 40 and 34. In addition Mrs. Holliday was a third grade teacher in the elementary school at Dayton Christian. No matter what the playing time of their athletes, the Holliday parents never complained and were very supportive of all the decisions we made all those years with their young men. I am thankful and proud of this family and it was a joy to work with them. James went on to be a principal and teacher at Dayton Christian. JT went on to be the head coach boys basketball of the varsity at Dayton Christian. The Hollidays are a model family and having four of their children play basketball for me was amazing.

If you have found yourself in the position of asking why my child is not playing during games or more importantly why my athlete has not gotten better, then this chapter is for you. Has this been a very frustrating experience for you and more importantly your athlete? Have you been cautioned or thrown out of your child's sporting events? Then this chapter is also for you.

"A St. Louis youth football coach is recovering from surgery after being shot four times by a disgruntled parent that was allegedly upset over his son's playing time, the St. Louis Metropolitan Police Department confirmed to *USA TODAY Sports*."[12]

"This is the latest incident of harassment and acts of violence toward youth coaches and umpires. In May, a Florida man was arrested for sucker-punching an umpire at his son's baseball game. Last year, a youth softball umpire in Mississippi was punched in the face by a mom."[13]

Frustrated Parents with Coaches

I know what it is like to be frustrated with the coaches because your athlete is not getting the right or desired playing time. Attacking or being abusive to coaches will not help and will not solve the issue of playing time. For example, when my son Kevin was a freshman playing baseball at Dayton Christian High School, I arrived back at the field to discover he had not played at all in a game. I approached Kevin after the game and asked him, "Did you play?" Kevin said no, so I approached the coach asking if there was a problem. Honestly speaking, my parent hat took over and that was a mistake on my part, and I should not have approached the coach right after the game especially since they lost. I should have contacted him the next day or so and asked for an appropriate time to speak with him. First, of all I knew the Dayton Christian participation policy was that every player that dresses will play in the game. I knew this policy as a coach and parent. The coach blew up at me but was fairer with Kevin after that. Oddly enough the coach changed Kevin's position from pitcher and first base to right field with no consideration to what position he had played in the past. The coach did this with the entire team rotating their positions on the Junior Varsity baseball team. After his freshman year of baseball Kevin was so frustrated that he did not play baseball again. I was sad that his baseball career ended like that, but he put all his energy into football.

As a parent that was my first time being frustrated with the fact that my son had gone to practice all week, done everything the coaching staff asked, showed up for the game and for whatever reason the coach decided not to put Kevin in the game. I asked Kevin a series of questions about why he did not play that day before I approached the coach including: Did you break a team rule? Did you miss a practice this week about which I did not know? Is the coach upset with you about something? Did the coach explain to you why you were not going to play today? The truth of the matter was the coach never even addressed Kevin and his playing time on that day. When I addressed the coach, he got defensive and aggressive saying, "Well he did not have his uniform belt today, he has not been hitting the ball well, and I need him to respond better to what I am trying to teach him." I told the coach that if Kevin had done something wrong why not be up front with him and let him know what the issue was verses ignoring him and acting unprofessional. That was his last season coaching baseball at Dayton Christian as the school terminated him at the end of the season because there were too many complaints from fans, parents, and players.

Have you become discouraged as a parent and is your athlete losing hope that they will ever get playing time? I am not sure how a coach expects a player to crack the rotation if they never evaluate the player and let them know specifically what they must do to get better. My senior year at McDonogh 35 was like that because coach Douglas only played seven to eight players a game no matter the score, win or lose. I sat on the bench game after game getting increasingly frustrated and we were losing a lot of games that season. I was at every practice, improved my game, worked on my deficiencies but coach Douglas just did not believe in playing a lot of players. The worst thing about it was he did not discuss with you how to get better. In addition, there was no player evaluation, so you were left to figure out how to improve your game on your own.

Has Your Athlete Earned More Playing Time?

I think one of the first questions a parent must ask if their athlete is in the situation of riding the pine is, does my athlete deserve to be on the bench? Secondly, is it possible that athletes getting more playing time than yours are simply more skilled and better athletes? If the answer is yes, then the parent has a responsibility to help their athlete gain the tools and skills to get better. The goal is to allow the athlete to have a positive rewarding experience in whatever sport they are playing to reach their athletic ceiling. Every player should know and be clear about their role on the team. Most parents never ask what the school or league policy on playing time is. Thirdly, what is the coach's policy regarding playing time? If an athlete is not mentally in the game, then there is a higher chance they will quit if their playing time is affected.[14] It frustrates me to see a coach is not playing players or putting players in a basketball game with thirty-two seconds left in the fourth quarter. As a parent you can help your athlete by knowing what their skill set is and having an appropriate expectation come game time. This will also help you as a parent to be a great cheerleader for your athlete and the team. In college we see so many players entering the transfer portal. Entering the transfer portal may not necessarily ensure your athlete gets better in their skill set. It may be worth careful consideration and considering the goal for the athlete.

Setting Your Athlete up for Success in Athletics and Academics

One of the most important things a parent can do is help prepare their athlete for their sport in the off season. How have you assisted your athlete in the offseason to prepare them for league play in the past? Are you relying on the coaches to get your athlete prepared during the actual season for competition? Have you taken the approach, "Well that is just not my job and that is why we have coaches?" This is a big misconception that many parents do not understand about coaching during the season. Most of the coach's focus is on practice and game preparation not on skill development during the season. Great coaches will give the athlete an offseason workout program and track how well they do. The University of Dayton football program was great at this as they had great incentive for players who attended offseason workouts. Kevin spent the spring of 2010 after transferring from Valparaiso University to the University of Dayton. Kevin made every workout at UD and won the iron-man award for completing every workout. Even though he was a collegiate athlete at this point and away from home I would encourage Kevin to attend these workouts.

I cannot emphasize enough that the off season is the time to get better and work on basic skills, not the regular season. For example, a coach's job is not to teach a player how to hold a basketball, how to dribble, how to shoot i.e., fundamentals during the season. Of course, I am talking about middle school and high school players. Elementary school players are an entirely different story because they have not had the time or years of experience to be that solid in their skills yet. These are the skill sets in basketball that a player should work on during the offseason. A parent does not have to know the game of basketball but can support the athlete by putting them in a bigger stronger faster program, teen weightlifting program, strength, and conditioning at the local YMCA for example. In addition, there are usually camps at the athlete's school, local colleges, and other locations to help the athlete work on skill sets that might need improvement. Many of these camps are not extremely expensive and can be of great benefit to the athlete. In addition, off-season conditioning and training offered by the local school should be attended by the athlete.

Also, I cannot stress how important academics and ACT or SAT test scores are in preparation for college. The results of all this challenging preparation for Kevin were academic scholarships to Miami University, University of Toledo, Bowling Green State University, Valparaiso University, and the University of Dayton. Kevin selected the Valparaiso University and was offered to join their football team and study Civil Engineering. This plan may seem extensive, but I can tell you it works and it paid off tremendously for Kevin. This plan gave Kevin the confidence mentally and physically to finish his senior year in high school and then play college football.

Please note that aside from athletics, academics, too, were an important part of Kevin's off-season schedule. Scholarships and financial assistance are always offered if needed. For example, the pre-engineering camp that Kevin attended at the University of Pittsburgh was via scholarship that included his tuition, room and board for the thirty-day academic camp. The key here is to investigate, and we have all the tools now with the internet and the ability to search the web for opportunities. Back then I Googled pre-engineering camps and that is how we found the camp at the University of Pittsburgh.

Kevin and I kept a journal of his off-season preparation and when he returned to school in August for his senior high school season, I was able to show his coach, Jamie Rice, all the work Kevin had put in to prepare for the upcoming season. I would then refer to the written evaluation that the coach had given us at the end of the last season to show how we addressed the areas he felt Kevin needed to improve upon and how faithful Kevin had been working on his game during the offseason months. The responses from the head and wide receiver coach was always incredibly positive. Dayton Christian was a running team as we had a two-thousand-yard rusher Kevin's sophomore and junior seasons. Kevin was still able to get his receiving yards, kickoff return yardage etc. More importantly Kevin improved his blocking skills and that kept him on the field. Kevin started every game from his sophomore to senior year at wide receiver and played quite a bit at cornerback. During Kevin's junior year we made the decision to hire NCSA (National Collegiate Scouting Association) to also represent Kevin in gaining a collegiate scholarship. This was also a great tool in getting Kevin's name out there since he attended a small high school.

By now you may be asking, "How do we really know what our athlete needs to work on to get better in the offseason?" That is the right question to ask. However, many coaches do not offer an end of season written player evaluation at the middle and high school levels. I always insisted on having one on my son Kevin to know specifically what he needed to work on in the offseason especially since I did not play football. His football coach was good at responding in writing when I asked him, "Coach, what do you think Kevin needs to work on in the offseason?" Once, we got that feedback from the coach in writing, I would speak with Kevin and together we laid out a plan from January—June when football workouts started. Kevin was an introvert, but I encouraged him to talk to his coaches and get to know them. This communication between player and coach was especially important for position as Kevin was a wide receiver and cornerback in high school. The offseason plan looked something like this:

Sample Football Offseason Workout Plan for Kevin, Junior Year 2008

1. January–June: Lift weights with football team Monday, Wednesday, Friday.
2. January–June: Cardio workout Tuesday and Thursday.
3. January–June: Catch one hundred passes, run various receiver routes three times a week. (Passes thrown by me)
4. May: Attended senior football camp at University Louisville.
5. June: Attended wide receiver/quarterback camp at Miami University.
6. June: 7 on 7 football camp Dayton Christian High School.
7. June: Attended the Nike camp at Notre Dame and met Charlie Weis, head football coach. Electronic 40-yard dash time.
8. June: Attended Nike Camp University of Toledo. Electronic 40-yard dash time.
9. June: ACT (academics), took ACT class in J-term at DC, practiced daily software program.
10. June: SAT (academics), took practice SAT test in October, practiced daily software program.
11. June: Senior Camp University Bowling Green State University. Electronic 40-yard dash time.
12. June: Senior Camp University of Cincinnati and met head football coach Brian Kelly.
13. June–July: Residence thirty-day program University of Pittsburgh Pre-Engineering Camp (academics).
14. August: Football week team camp—Athletes in Action Xenia, Ohio.
15. August: Fall football practice began.
16. July–August: Ran wide receiver routes and caught one hundred passes a week (thrown by me).

17. Chose ten colleges and complete applications submitted in August.
18. Hired NCSA (National Collegiate Scouting Association) to represent Kevin.
19. After ten college visits he chose Valparaiso University in February 2009.

Parent Tip 12
Parents should be familiar with the Institution's Athletic Handbook on policies and procedures, especially playing time.

Parent Tip 13
Parents should build a positive relationship with their athletes' coaches, athletic director, and school officials. When you go to visit it is important to ask the coach questions so you can build a better understanding of who they are and how they like to run their program.[15]

Parent Tip 14
Develop an action plan no later than the athlete's sophomore year of high school to include goals for academics and athletics. This should include the athlete, coaching staff, and parents. Track the plan and provide updates to the coaching staff. Do not be afraid to reach out to college coaches in that sophomore year.

Parent Tip 15
Use social media as a positive tool to get exposure for your athlete to perspective colleges. Send game films and high school transcripts. Always post the best two or three game plays of the week. Do not seek "Likes" on social media. This is strictly for prospective colleges or universities. Technology has been used as a means of both regulating and controlling behavior as well as a means of circumventing that regulation and control.[16]

Proverbs 15:22 "Plans fail for lack of counsel, but with many advisers they succeed." NIV

"I'll do whatever it takes to win games, whether it's sitting on a bench waving a towel, handing a cup of water to a teammate or hitting the game-winning shot."
Kobe Bryant

Pro-tip From Coach Rome

It takes more than athletic talent to be a college athlete, let alone be an athlete on scholarship. Your child's grades matter and they matter a lot. Athletes who combine great grades with talent (and a good attitude) will get the best offers from college coaches. [17]

5 How to Stay Involved

Wendell (middle) in Iraq at the Joint Base Balad hospital with American Gladiators Titan (left) and Destroyer (right), 2008.

Let me first say I empathize with you as a parent if you have a job that requires travel. Do not be discouraged about this. Over 460 million people travel for business annually in the U.S. This is a massive 150% increase from 2020 when there were only 185 million, and similar to 2019s numbers.[18] In this same article I found some affirming statistics about parent travelers to confirm my point for the need of this chapter. These travelers tend to fall under certain demographics, with at least 50% of business travelers between the ages of 35-54 and 56% of business travelers holding professional or managerial positions that earn at least $127,000 per year.[19] You can still be a huge part of your athlete's life if deployed or working away from home all the time.

From 2008–2009 I was deployed for about nine months during that time frame. This was unusual because with the National Guard, I was typically away from home three days a month. In 2008, I was first deployed to the Island of Guam for three months. I returned home and got a phone call from the Air National Guard Chaplains office saying they needed my hospital skills as a hospital chaplain in Iraq at Joint Base Balad as the senior hospital chaplain. Alesia was home off work during that time, which was a good thing. The huge issue was that Kevin was headed into his senior football season as a standout wide receiver and was being heavily recruited by many colleges.

Do Not Let Guilt Guide You in Supporting Your Athlete

Have you ever felt guilty about having to miss your child's school play, sporting event or spelling bee? Was the reason you missed the event due to your job insisting that you travel, and it could not be avoided? Work travel gets exponentially harder as a parent of a young kid—doubly so if your partner also travels for work, and even harder if you're a single parent.[20] But work travel isn't something you have to avoid as a parent, it's just something that you manage as best you can and then pick up the pieces when best laid plans fall apart.[21] When parents must travel, it can eat away at your spirit. It took me awhile to learn how to be present when I was always away from home. I adopted the concept of being a proactive parent no matter where I was. In Bill Beausay's book *Teenage Boys*, he suggests six principles of being a proactive parent that I have found helpful:

1. Don't just be there; be audaciously present.
2. Don't try to force change—provoke it.
3. Don't just have a good attitude; get a great metaphor.

4. Don't tolerate teens; get passionate about them.
5. Don't get a bigger hammer; get a better idea.
6. Have fun.

Since Kevin was in seventh grade, I had only missed one or two of his football games. The deployment to Iraq would mean I'd miss the entire football season as a parent and also as the football team chaplain. We made the tough decision to accept the deployment, but I needed a plan to show my continued support of Kevin during the most crucial time in his life. Honestly, I dreaded the deployment after twenty-nine years of military service because the timing was just terrible but when is the timing right for the deployment? I felt several emotions including guilt, but Kevin reassured me constantly that he was fine and doing well. I learned over the years that missing one or two of my children's games or events was not that critical in the big scheme of our relationship or parenting. I tried to mirror a splendid example of a father and husband being present although sometimes I was not physically present. I was there always in spirit.

I got on the airplane in August 2008 praying everyone would be okay, especially Kevin. A note to parents is to trust the work and efforts you put in to help your athlete. It was time for me to take a page from my favorite sayings "Do your best and trust God with the Rest." Kevin did make it through his senior season. Alesia took Kevin on his first visit to Valparaiso to check out the school and team. I made it through the deployment, but Kevin did not have as good of a season as his junior year in football. In the end, however, we had a good plan and Kevin felt loved and supported. I felt connected to him, and we did the best we could as a family through a challenging time. I hear all the time students saying their parents chose their college and major and they hated it. I did not agree with Kevin's choice of college. I wanted him to attend a DIII school like Oberlin or Kenyon College. In the end I accepted that it was Kevin's choice, and my job was to support his decision. His decision was not a bad one, I just felt a smaller college would better suit him. This taught me a valuable lesson in that attending Kevin's games was important, but it was never about me it was about him. *New York Times* columnist Parker-Pope notes that focusing too much on a child's sports schedule can send the message that the children are playing for us and not for themselves.[22]

It is never too early to start educating and supporting your athlete about college or life after high school. I fear that parents spend so much time and effort on AAU and club sports hoping for an athletic scholarship, only to find out full rides are not offered in those sports at all colleges. We decided to hire a recruiting firm, the National Collegiate Scouting Association. This was expensive (under $4,000) but worthwhile for both Kevin and me. Once Kevin decided on Valparaiso for the summer of his senior year, he got his work out plan and playbook from them. Kevin was a wide receiver in high school was 6'1 and weighed 185 which I felt was light for college ball. I hired an athletic trainer from the University of Dayton basketball team which costs about $1500 to work with Kevin three days a week. Kevin was also doing job shadowing at the Department of Veterans Affairs engineering service where I worked. I would take him to UD at 8am and he would work with the trainer for an hour. I would go back to UD to pick him up and then we would both work at the VA. On the way back we would stop at McDonald's and get Kevin two McGriddles and chocolate milk. He had to take in so many extra calories a day to put on muscle and weight. At the end of the summer, he had put on ten pounds of muscle and looked great at 195 lbs. If it is not possible for you to hire a trainer, your local YMCA offers programs for your athlete that are quite inexpensive. A sample deployment plan is on the next page for military families or families where the parent will be away from home for an extensive period of time:

Sample Parent/Child Athletics Deployment Plan

- I looked up the football schedule for the season and began thinking about how I could support Kevin while in Iraq.
- I researched all the teams on the schedule through the internet to look at schedules, defense, defenders, cornerbacks, and safeties who might be defending Kevin. Keep in mind this was 2008 and social media was not what it is today yet there was information on the teams' websites etc.
- While in Iraq I made DVDs after studying all the information on what Kevin could expect, reminded him of his strengths and encouraged him to do his best. I ended each DVD conversation with a prayer and told him I loved him.
- His mother would make sure that each night before Kevin went to bed he would listen to the DVDs. On Thursday, I would try to call home when I could before each Friday game. I would always end our conversation with, "I am proud of you," and "I love you."
- While in Iraq, every Wednesday, on my day off from the hospital, I would read a story to Kevin and Destiny and make it age appropriate for both. This was on two separate DVDs lasting about twenty minutes each. I would encourage Kevin and give life lessons from books. Morale Welfare and Recreation would then package the DVDs and mail them to Trotwood, Ohio, where we lived. Morale Welfare and Recreation had a special program where you could come in and use their video equipment and they would mail your DVD to your family.
- Also, while in Iraq, I would mail Kevin a card with a few dollars to let him know I was thinking of him. I mailed Destiny Beanie Babies that I would get from the Base Exchange.
- Another parent sent me DVDs of Kevin's football games to Iraq. I did not offer any critical feedback to Kevin. I simply enjoyed the games and was blessed by them.
- Kevin and I talked by phone weekly about the communication he was having with coaches regarding the recruiting process, and I would pass on any information I received as well.
- I would write and call my other sons, Wendell and Keaton, while on the deployment also.

Parent Tip 16

Communicate with your athlete as much as possible while you are away from home at least weekly. Do what you can. Use all tools of communication that are safe, private, and available to you and your athlete. This should be frequent, especially in the recruiting stage of their career. Also remember to be a parent and end every conversation with an expression of love. Let these conversations be positive and encouraging. Stay involved. Plan. Be proactive. Make the events you can and do not worry about the ones you miss.

Parent Tip 17

When reintegrating back home from deployment or long business trip, do have a reintegration plan. A notable example was me not agreeing with Kevin's choice of college. I accepted his decision and then did what I could to support his transition to college. I trusted the plans we had put in place pre-deployment, during deployment and when I returned home.

Titus 2:7 "In everything set them an example by doing what is good." *ESV*

Pro-tip From Coach Rome

Humor is a great tool when talking to your athlete. I was watching a tape of one of Kevin's football games in 2008 while in Iraq and quoted John McKay of the Tampa Bay Buccaneers who in 1976 went 0-14. "We didn't tackle well today but we made up for it by not blocking." I told Kevin, "Have fun and remember football is just a game. You did not drop that pass it just hit your hands the wrong way."

6 Never Focus On Winning or Losing

Summer 2022, 10U Kleptz YMCA basketball team.

🔔 Sometimes You Must Lose to Win Again!

After losing in the 10U regional tournament for three seasons, winter and summer 2022–2023, the Kleptz Notre Dame Fighting Irish in Englewood, Ohio, won the YMCA regional tournament with a perfect 13–0 season. The summer of 2022 we did not even win a game in our local tournament. It was the first time in all my years coaching that I did not have a player not call or show up but our point guard did just that. We continued to be faithful and build our skills over the next three seasons. The winter season 2024 was amazing and my only undefeated season. It was an emotional day for us as we played three games on Saturday March 16, 2024. The second game we played was against Kettering South who was the team that knocked us out of the tournament those two previous seasons. We would not be denied and therefore beat Kettering South 48–24. We went into the season with a purpose, which was to get back to the regional tournament and prove to ourselves that we had improved as a team. The fact that we lost those previous three seasons taught us how to win. Although losing was painful, it prepared us for winning. Not one time in the season did I talk about winning or losing. All we talked about was being faithful individually and as a team. I was so proud of the team because they learned the true meaning of Winning Is the Result of Being Faithful. Many athletes question why they should work hard if their team isn't going to succeed regardless.[23]

Ecclesiastes 9:11 "I have observed something else under the sun. The fastest runner doesn't always win the race, and the strongest warrior doesn't always win the battle. The wise sometimes go hungry, and the skillful are not necessarily wealthy. And those who are educated don't always lead successful lives. It is all decided by chance, by being in the right place at the right time." *NIV*

All Goals, From Coaching to Athletics and Parenting Athletes, Should Include Being Faithful

Depending on what level a coach is coaching, their goal is typically to win. In Chapter One, we talked about what is a coach's purpose for coaching and that coaching is a calling. In sports, a great question is what is the difference between a goal and a purpose? A goal is a specific objective we want to accomplish.[24] On the other hand, answer life's larger questions not, "What do I do today?" but, "Why do I exist?" and, "What are my functions in life?"[25]

"Winning isn't everything, it's the only thing." This infamous quote, often attributed to Vince Lombardi, actually originated with college football coach Red Sanders, though Lombardi did say it as well.[26] A second well-known quote, "Winning is only valuable when it is accomplished *in the right way.*"[27] Several years ago I was traveling doing National Guard duty and was on a layover flying from Dayton, Ohio, to Des Moines, Iowa. To kill time before my next flight, I stopped in a shop in O'Hare Airport. I did something I had never done. I bought a book in the airport called *The ONE Thing* by Gary W. Keller and Jay Papasan. Coaches at every level seem to believe that winning is the only thing that matters. I understand coaching is some individuals' main source of income and the difference between winning and losing could cost them their job. I decided a long time ago for me athletic coaching had to be about more than winning. After reading *The ONE Thing*, my position on coaching was reaffirmed. Be like a postage stamp—stick to one thing until you get there.[28] The one thing for me in coaching and in life is to focus on being faithful. In life this has served me well. For example, in the military, I enlisted as an E-1 Airman basic and finished my career as an 0–5 Lieutenant Colonel. People asked me how I did it and they are shocked at my response. I just tried to be faithful throughout my thirty-five-year military career. I did not say it was always easy but somehow this philosophy has served me well professionally and also in coaching athletics.

I was coaching the Dayton Christian freshman team in 2005–2006. That year we were not particularly, good however we won half our games in the Metro Buckeye league in Dayton, Ohio. To this point I had not lost a lot of players to academic ineligibility, especially coaching at a private school. I was determined not to lose any players that year because we were thin, especially at point guard. We had a point guard named Joe Homes who was particularly good, and we moved him up to spend some time on the Junior Varsity. When the first quarter grades came out, he was academically ineligible despite my efforts to talk to parents, teachers, and the players about being faithful with their grades.

Dayton Christian Basketball 9th grade team 2nd place finishers at Northridge Christmas Tournament, 2nd place at the Metro Buckeye Conference, 2005–2006.

At the end of the school year, he transferred to Wayne High School in Huber Heights, Ohio, and I am not sure how he faired out there, but I know he graduated on time. Fast forward to the fall of 2021, I was sitting in my class at the University of Dayton School of Law and this same student walked in. We embraced in joy. The other students were wondering what was going on and we told them the story. He joined the Navy after high school, getting his education while serving and did well enough on the LSAT to get accepted into Law School. We graduated together in May 2022, and what a privilege it was to know this young man and to have been a part of his journey. This is one reason I believe in teaching athletes to be faithful to the things that really matter and not to merely focus on the wins and losses. It may have seemed like he lost in his freshman year, but he is a winner today because he understands the meaning of being faithful. I like how the songwriter Fantasia puts it in her hit song, "Sometimes you have to lose to win again." What a wonderful example of how in high school this athlete did not understand the concept of *Winning Is the Result of Faithfulness*, but he did get it later and is now a practicing attorney and a basketball coach.

Other challenges are, what happens when the athlete is tired of losing and wants to quit the sport? What happens if the athlete gets injured and must quit the sport? Just ask the 70% of young athletes that quit because it just wasn't fun anymore.[29] What happens when the athlete has a terrible experience with a coach and wants to quit the sport? What happens when so much focus has been put on winning that the athlete is turned off by sports? I like the article in *Psychology Today* by Warrick Wood, "Maintaining a Winning Focus is Not the Way to Win" that talks about the uncontrollable vs controllable aspects of competition. Athletes, coaches, and support staff can do everything in their power to prepare for competition; however, the nature of sport provides to many uncontrollable elements (referees, weather, opposition, equipment, etc.) that can influence the outcome for the dominant focus to be on that end state."[30] Some say focus on performance and the outcome of the game will be fine. I say focus on being faithful and the outcome of the game will be fine. I have a policy during the regular season to not discuss winning and losing with my teams. Our focus is on learning what it means to be faithful. God willing when we get to the tournament, playing faithfully will equal wins at a time that really matters.

In youth sports, most of the time, all teams play in the end of season tournament. While seeding may be important at the youth level, any team can win on any given day. In other words, it is very fluid and just because you were the best team in the regular season does not mean you will win your tournament. I also tell my teams to not look at the scoreboard at half time. If we are winning by a lot or if it is a close game, it does not matter because we still have another half of basketball to play. I want the team to be focused and remain faithful for four quarters not just two.

🏷️ Remember the Titans

I have seen many great sports movies over the years that I really liked such as *Facing the Giants,* a Christian movie about football, and *Remember the Titans,* which was based on a true story and won eight awards and seventeen movie nominations. It was one of my favorites because it focused on the social aspect of building a team and being faithful. In one scene in the movie a running back keeps fumbling, so the dad tapes the football with duct tape around the athlete's hands and totally humiliates him. The running back's father had played for the school and was an outstanding player who had grand expectations for his son which the movie portrayed as unrealistic. The dad was not only an off-the-hook parent but at times seemed verbally and physically abusive if his son did not perform to *his* standards. The father only cared about one thing—winning. His son played hurt like many athletes do from direct or indirect peer pressure. They must play hurt and if they aren't willing to play through injury, says the old foolish adage, then they don't care about their team. Children focused solely on winning are more likely to play through an injury, thus risking further or even permanent damage.[31]

How do we move away from a "winning is everything" mentality and instead focus on development, performance, and faithfulness? The key is threefold: having organizations, parents, and coaches on the same page. The coach is the key. Coaches are on the front line in defining what success is in athletics and how it transcends to life skills. Parents should know the history of the coach's *ego* and how they handle losing! A coach cannot just be a good witness when they win, it is more important to role model a great witness in losing. An athlete should never believe that winning at all costs is more important than academics, citizenship or enjoying the game. The last thing I tell my players in our pre-game talk is, "Make sure you have fun and enjoy the game!" This used to be an old school model but working at the YMCA

I have talked to many athletes who cannot seem to stay on the court or field because their focus is on all the wrong places. They have been taught that winning is all that matters. They have not been taught to be faithful and this is something that must change because there is a reality in sports. Please, look at the reality of collegiate scholarships and sports in the four bullet points below, "according to the NCAA." www.NCAA.org/playcollegesports.

- Does the NCAA award athletics scholarships? Individual schools award athletics scholarships. Divisions I and II schools provide $2.7 billion in athletic scholarships annually to more than 150,000 student-athletes. Division III schools, with more than 180,000 student-athletes, do not offer athletically related financial aid, but many student-athletes receive some form of academic grant or need-based scholarship.
- Do many high school athletes earn athletics scholarships? Very few, in fact. About 2 percent of high school athletes are awarded some form of athletics scholarship to compete in college.
- Do NCAA student-athletes have difficulty meeting graduation requirements with the demands of their sport? While competing in college does require strong time-management skills and some thoughtful planning with academic advisors, on average NCAA student-athletes graduate at a higher rate than the general student body.
- Do many NCAA student-athletes go on to play professionally? Fewer than 2 percent of NCAA student-athletes go on to be professional athletes. Most student-athletes depend on academics to prepare them for life after college. Education is important. There are more than 460,000 NCAA student-athletes, and most of them will go pro in something other than sports.

Parent Tip 18

The one thing in athletics that parents must teach their athletes is to be faithful, win or lose. In other words, learning how to lose is critical and all about attitude. Losing can be a blessing and encourages opportunity for growth and further development in being faithful.

2 Timothy 2:5 "An athlete is not crowned unless he competes according to the rules." *ESV*

"Success demands singleness of purpose." *Vince Lombardi*

Parent Tip 19

Parents should ensure that their athletes never believe that winning at all costs is more important than academics, citizenship or enjoying the game.

"You are not defeated when you lose. You are defeated when you quit." *Paulo Coelho*

"When you lose, talk little. When you win, talk less." *Tom Brady*

"If you want to be an athlete, then getting good grades, going to college, and developing your intellectual skills are important." *Tony Dungy*

Pro-tip From Coach Rome

One of the lies that gets in athlete's heads is that losing is okay and not to dream big. I say do not let losing get in your spirit and it is okay to dream big. Do not get comfortable with losing, but continue being faithful. Give your best effort and trust God with the rest.

7 Parent Code of Conduct

14U Northmont SAY Soccer team (Lauren, fourth player, back row, from right), 2018.

Parents have been given a tremendous amount of responsibility to raise their children. All the organizations I have coached for have Codes of Conduct. "A code of conduct is a short document that outlines expected behaviors of everyone at your organization."[32] Although parents, coaches and athletes acknowledge the code during registration with signatures, severe violations continue to occur. Every season I see a parent, athlete or coach violating these codes that harm athletes or officials. The reason is not a lack of policies but a lack of consistency with enforcing the codes of conduct. For example, at the YMCA before every sporting event we make a pledge by the players on both teams to obey the Codes of Conduct.

🐚 The Sportsmanship Announcement Is Not Just for the Players, It Is for the Parents and Fans Also

The YMCA sports pledge states the following: "I pledge to play to the best of my ability. To be loyal to my teammates. Show courtesy to my opponents, spectators, and officials. I will show good sportsmanship and fair play." As the sports site supervisor I had to remind athletes, coaches, and parents of the Sports Pledge and that the YMCA is a Christian organization. Every time I have said that to someone, they look at me cross eyed like they have no clue what I am talking about. I have witnessed this every where I have coached over the years and it is quite appalling. In addition, I recall when coaching high school basketball in Ohio the announcer would announce the Ohio athletic association rules for parents and fans before each high school game.

An example is a mother of my 2018 Northmont 14U soccer team (pictured on the previous page) cussing out a fourteen-year-old referee during our soccer game. The league managers were called to the field, and she cussed them all out also. I was shocked. Parents told me this was normal behavior for that parent, she does it every year. Another example; after a 2011 basketball game at Miami Valley School in Dayton, I was in the parking lot, and I could overhear a father scolding his son who had played in the game. Their school lost the game, but I thought the athlete was faithful and played well in that loss. The dad told him, "You are a disgrace and have embarrassed me." He went on to say, "I am ashamed of you." It got so bad that I intervened and asked the man to please not do this to his son and that his behavior was inappropriate. Of course, the dad told me to mind my own business. I could not let it go and the next day I told our athletic director at the school, and he passed on the incident to the athlete's school. The response from the other school was gratitude, and they said they would address the situation. It was not the first time, it turns out, that this father had attacked his son in this fashion. The parent code of conduct is therefore not just between the parent and the organization but also for the protection of the athlete and officials or referees.

I recall reading a story when I was preparing for a sermon where a young boy followed his father's pattern of communication. Every morning while the father was driving the boy to school the father would engage in road rage calling all the other drivers idiots. One day at school the boy got upset with his teacher and told her, "You are just like the idiot drivers we see every morning." When the principal at the school asked the boy where he learned such language he said, "Oh my father calls all the drivers every morning idiots." The sportsmanship young athletes show on the field starts at home with their parents. Coaches coach and try to set a good example of sportsmanship most of the time. However, coaches teach athletes to be physical, aggressive and we love saying we must punch the other team in the mouth. You may have noticed in football games at all levels all the talking going on between the players and referees.

Typically, this conversation is encouraged with the team captains to speak on behalf of the team, but each player is not supposed to complain to the referees on every play about something. Young athletes watch professional sports and mimic what they see these athletes doing. Sometimes, as in the case of high school football player Emmanuel Duran, this example leads to tragedy. Emmanuel Duran lost control of his temper in a football game in Edinburg, Texas. A high school football player in Texas became infamous when he did the unthinkable, leveling a referee.[33] Emmanuel was arrested that night and spent the night in jail. He is now trying to put the pieces back together after this incident in 2019. Emmanuel charging and tackling the referee was a result of him talking to the referee throughout the game and when he was ejected from the game he lost control and no one could hold him back. I do wish Emmanuel the best and hope he can get his life back on track but I watch games every week on television and sometimes I am afraid things will get out of hand on the field.

On the court is a different story and I have a rule. My basketball players do not talk to the referees unless spoken to and that includes not complaining about calls. This also includes non-verbal language like throwing your hands in the air when the referee makes a call. What makes it hard when you are trying to instill respect and discipline in your players is the parents on the sideline yelling obscene comments at the referees even at youth sporting events. I heard recently here in Ohio how at a Trotwood Madison High School girls game parents came out of the stands and fought with female athletes who were playing in a basketball game. According to witnesses, an incident broke out when players from both sides went after a loose ball.[34] A few fans reportedly came onto the court and players from each team left the bench to go onto the court.[35] More than ten players were reportedly ejected from the game.[36] Of course, this incident was posted immediately on the internet, and it went viral. The approval and likes were very disappointing to me.

If parents cannot act accordingly at sporting events, it is exceedingly difficult for athletes to control themselves. A basketball game or sporting event is not a reality show. I am praying that parents will understand and honor the Code of Conduct and in the future get back to the one thing in athletics that really matters. The one thing that should really matter with parents and their athletes is teaching them to be "faithful." In other words, how we play the game should still matter. An athlete's reputation does matter, and colleges and professional teams are becoming less tolerant of players who do not understand or want to be held accountable for their poor actions. I am hopeful with organizations understanding compliance and a zero tolerance with parents that do not follow the Code of Conduct is the way to go and essential for the integrity of sports. Compliance is the key and the moment a parent breaks the Code of Conduct it must be addressed. On the following page is a sample Parent Code of Conduct that every parent must sign.

Sample Parent Code of Conduct

The following guidelines have been created to meet the standards, policies, and procedures of the XYZ organization. Please read the Parent Code of Conduct below and sign:

- Please communicate with the staff daily, if possible.
- Do come visit our program and have fun with your child; you are always welcome.
- Do give detailed information to the Program Director if custody situations arise.
- People whose behavior and/or health status pose an immediate threat or danger to the health and safety of the children must not be present when children are in care.
- Do not confront any child in a threatening manner or confront children from other families.
- Using profanity in the presence of a minor is prohibited and against the law.
- In the event of threatening behavior towards a staff member or child, 911 will be called.
- Consumption, and/or possession of alcohol in any form is strictly prohibited. Controlled substances/medications must be accompanied by a written doctor's prescription when used during the program, during transportation, or on field trips. People must not be under the influence of or impaired by alcohol or controlled substances in the program, during transportation, or on field trips.
- Children will not be released to parents, guardians, or other authorized individuals if the staff feels as though the individual is consuming, under the influence or impaired by alcohol or a controlled substance.
- People must not smoke or use tobacco products at the child-care center, on the premises, on the playground, in transportation vehicles or during field trips.
- Parents should exercise good judgment when posting comments on any social media platform regarding players, other coaches, institutions, or athletic officials.
- Parents are expected to own and repair any mistakes made online. Do this in a new post; do not just correct the old post.

CONSEQUENCES OF PARENT MISBEHAVIOR: Violations of any of the above results in the parent's removal from the building, police being contacted, or the child's removal from our program.

Parent Tip 20
Parents should be encouraged not to post fights or disruptive player behavior on social media. The event going viral is not helpful. Parents should also encourage their kids or athletes not to post these events on social media either.

Parent Tip 21
Organizations must adopt a zero tolerance with parents who choose to not follow the Code of Conduct. Enforcing compliance for organizations is the key.

Proverbs 15:4 "A gentle tongue is a tree of life, but perverseness in it breaks the spirit." *NIV*

Principles Parents Can Model to their Athletes

- If you lose, do not make excuses.
- If you win, win humbly.
- If you make a mistake, do not get down on yourself, get back in the game.
- Always do your best and trust God with the rest.
- If a teammate, coach, or official makes a mistake, remain encouraging and do not criticize.
- Always show respect for the game and everyone involved.
- Remember, sports are a game at all levels.

Pro-tip From Coach Rome
Parents, please realize what is newsworthy in the life of your athlete when posting on social media and do not solicit LIKES!

8 Coaches Code of Conduct

Kleptz YMCA winter junior high school team, 2024.

🏀 You Can Not Just Show Sportsmanship When You Win

In the Winter 2024, I coached two basketball teams at the Kleptz YMCA. The junior high team that is pictured above and the 10U team that is pictured in other parts of the book. It was my first time working with this group of junior high seventh and eighth grade athletes. They were a great group of athletes but it was challenging teaching them the concept of Winning Is the Result of Faithfulness. However, midway in the season they began to believe. We began to be faithful especially in our defense. We played the first place team and beat them by fifteen points. This team had not lost a game in three years. Ironically, they would be the same team we would play in our first tournament game at the Kleptz YMCA in March 2024. We could not practice the week of the game due to the gym not being available. The rule is no outside or unsanctioned practices from the YMCA. This coach wanted to win so badly he held a practice offsite and installed a 2-1-2 defense to shut down our scoring and it worked; we lost the game by four points. Sometimes in athletics you win on the scoreboard but you lose the overall game. I was very saddened when I learned the coach had cheated and held an extra practice. He violated one of the rules of the Coaching Code of Conduct and many other policies of the YMCA just to win. It is important for coaches to show great sportsmanship even if they lose the game.

In Chapter Seven I talked about the Parent Code of Conduct. I am now transitioning to the Coach's Code of Conduct which is equally important. This code of conduct is typically between the organization the coach is working for, the parents and the athletes. An effective Code of Conduct lets you set aside worries about unsportsmanlike conduct and allows you to stay focused on the positives of youth and community. I believe a Coach's Code of Conduct is a contract. Dictionary.com defines a contract as an agreement between two or more parties for doing or not doing something specified.

Zero Tolerance

A Coach's Code of Conduct could cover many things from the minor, such as player playing time, on up to much more serious offenses like inappropriate coach player relationships. I have developed many relationships with coaches over the years and we root for each other. When you compete against certain coaches you develop a special relationship. That was the case when I met a coach from Troy Christian High School. We became close and coached against each other for three years. Once, while chatting for a few minutes before a game in their gym, I noticed several female students approaching him. They were flirting, which raised some red flags in my mind. As a friend, I told him, "You must be careful. Set boundaries with these female students." Coaches remember to encourage and support each other. Coaching can be a lonely, isolated path even when you are extraordinarily successful.

Later, I was disappointed but not surprised to learn that he had a criminal case against him and was being charged with sexual assault. I am sure you noticed this was at a Christian School and it did not seem to make much difference. The coach was convicted of Felony Sexual Battery for sexual conduct with a fifteen-year-old girl and was sentenced to five years in prison for the sexual crime. "Jury selection got started today, Sept. 1, in the Miami County trial of a former Troy Christian School coach accused of setting fire to his home within days of his 2007 indictment for sexual conduct with a teen-age girl."[37] He was married to an Army soldier and his son played on the varsity basketball team. Our league was rocked by what happened and to this day I am still saddened by what happened. He was a great basketball coach and I doubt he ever coached again after his convictions.

I have no doubt this coach signed a Coaching Code of Conduct. The Christian Schools tend to be stricter on who they let coach, but I explained to them over the years that their focus is not always in the right place with compliance. For example, in 2004 when I first applied to coach at Dayton Christian, they rejected me because I had been divorced. There was a policy at the school that if you had been through a divorce no matter what the circumstances you could not coach. I petitioned the school and was successful in getting them to change this policy and examine each coach's history a little closer versus a blanket no. My argument was that as a chaplain in the Air National Guard and serving as a chaplain in the Department of Veterans Affairs I had been through every background check, met every clergy board, been examined, and scrutinized and found to be acceptable to serve. So, if I was cleared to serve in the military and

VA in ministry, I should be able to coach at a christian school. They agreed with me, and that opened the door at Dayton Christian for other coaches who were great coaches to be able to coach. Oddly, we have background checks and must be certified by the state of Ohio to coach middle and high school basketball in Ohio. Compliance with coaches' behavior is left to the schools or organizations. I was concerned about the aforementioned coach's behavior and even brought it to the attention of our head basketball coach. He passed on our concerns to the Troy Christian Athletic director but like most sexual abusers, the coach was very charming.

I would encourage every organization to protect the children, coaches, and organization by using a Coaching Code of Conduct. A big issue today is social media and all the different platforms such as cell phones, Instagram, Facebook, Tik-Tok, Messenger etc. Wisdom is the key here and coaches need to be able to identify potential risks and follow policies that help them identify problem areas before they strike. A coach is discouraged from communicating at the YMCA with players on any of these platforms, yet I am sure some coaches still do it. Once, while coaching SAY soccer U10, I overheard an assistant coach ask one of the girls, "Did you get my message on Facebook?" I informed him that this was inappropriate and not tolerated by Trotwood SAY soccer because I did not want him to get into trouble. I am not sure if he listened to my feedback, but I have tried to caution coaches over the years about boundaries with parents and especially the athletes.

🏐 Training and Mentorship Support for Coaches

Training and mentorship for coaches is a critical component to getting them to understand the nature of their job and the expectations of the organization in serving the athletes they will be coaching. When I was coaching school ball in the state of Ohio, all coaches at the middle and high school level had to go through the PUPIL Activity certification

Coach Rome and Coach Brittani, Kleptz 10U winter basketball league champions, 2023.

to be a state certified coach. As one of the sports site supervisors at the Kleptz YMCA in Englewood, Ohio, we have background checks. In addition, we must take courses in Appropriate/age-appropriate outside contact, Alone Time, Child Sexual Abuse, Appropriate Touch, Slips/Trips/Falls, Bloodborne Pathogens and of course First Aid/CPR. Injuries will occur and a coach needs to be prepared to deal with that athlete at places like the YMCA because there is no athletic trainer to care for the athletes. Just this past year I had one female player break a finger, a boy had a concussion and several minor knee injuries. Blood is on players every game that we must get cleaned up so play can continue. Most organizations do an excellent job with this training but offer little if anything on how to coach the athletes. There are typical practice plans for practice, but the managing of a ball game is so different. The answer here may be for organizations to pair new coaches up with a willing mentor in the organization who might be able to guide them in their new role. The picture of my 2023 winter 10U team shows one of the coach's I have mentored over the years. Coach Brittani is a wonderful coach and I hope she will continue coaching athletics for some years to come.

Coaches need to be honest with themselves. Everyone cannot work with other people's children even in high school. Parents, guardians etc. should be in constant contact with their athlete to ensure they feel safe, encouraged, and are enjoying their experience on the team. My high school coach played favorites, often to the detriment of the team. Inferior players saw playing time while better players, like me, sat on the bench. It was mentally challenging to sit game after game watching the same poor coaching and management. Parents need to be involved and not over trust the organization or the coach. More teachers, coaches, and mentors have destroyed the hopes and dreams of young athletes or students by merely saying negative words to them. It was a mental game with Coach Doug in high school and I am not sure he meant to work his players over that way, but it did happen. I am sure many athletes left our basketball team at McDonogh 35 and never played hoops again.

Gaslighting in Coaching Athletes

Coach Doug used gaslighting by psychologically manipulating players such as giving certain players the best gear, not talking to us unless we were a starter, or not acknowledging us as part of the team. Although coach Doug did not cut any players he did have his favorite players on the team. For example, we had fourteen players on the team, and he only gave t-shirts to ten players. I felt left out, disrespected and that he didn't really consider me a part of the team. Many coaches find themselves in the headlines for all the wrong reasons. I have read and seen reports of how the legendary Bob Knight, though a wonderful coach, was extremely hard and sometimes abusive verbally and physically with his basketball players. Other modern-day coaches are facing similar challenges. At the end of 2018, the University of Maryland investigated a football coach for intimidation, humiliation and verbal abuse.[38] This followed a player dying of heat stroke after a training session on a 41°C day.[39] Earlier that year, UK swimmer Karen Leach revealed the long-term impact of what she said was sexual, mental, physical and emotional abuse inflicted on her by a former Olympic coach when she was a young swimmer.[40] A study of 12 former child athletes in the United Kingdom showed most had been frequently threatened and humiliated—part of emotional abuse.[41] These were former athletes across several sports including diving, football, gymnastics, hockey, netball, and track and field athletics.[42] I do not know how many schools coaches are guilty of gaslighting their athletes. Kevin was shocked by the level of profanity and other player/coach communication when he transitioned from Dayton Christian to Valparaiso. It was a difficult transition for him, and I believe contributed to him making the decision to quit football. Parents should ask questions about each coach and ask the coach what is their communication style? Do they yell, use profanity, how do they discipline players? If that is not possible then find out as much as you can about the history of the school and the coaching staff. Usually, if a coach is a gaslighter there will be some history that they have done this everywhere they have been.

    The last point in this chapter is that of coaching conduct. In high school some coaches use profanity with the referees. When I was at The Miami Valley School, we played Alter High School, and it was a great game. We were winning by ten points but could not make a free throw. The Alter coach was very experienced but cussed each referee out until he finally got a technical foul. He did all that cussing with a priest on the bench who travels with the team. Even as a military man I had not heard such profanity in my entire life. In my thirty-three years coaching I have received only one technical foul. I was coaching the freshman team at The Miami Valley School, and we were playing at Cincinnati Christian High School. In a heated game a loose ball came to me, and I caught it and slammed it on the floor. I learned that day to keep my emotions in check and how sensitive referees can be. We won that game by one point, but the technical foul could have cost us the game. I apologized to my players and parents and informed the school that I had received the technical foul. That was the first and last time I ever had an encounter with an official. My philosophy now is to focus on my players and manage the game. I trust in our preparation and if we are faithful that should equate success. There are good and bad calls in a sporting event but players and coaches being faithful should not change. As coaches we cannot choose good sportsmanship only when we win, it is also important when we lose.

Sample Coaches Code of Conduct

Youth sports should offer competitive fun in a values-oriented, healthy, and fair play environment. I WILL:

- Provide a playing environment for my players that is safe from physical and emotional harm.
- Do my best to be knowledgeable of the rules and fundamentals of the game and teach them to my players.
- Complete required child abuse prevention training and attend a coaches meeting to familiarize myself with YMCA policies, procedures, and emergency response plans.
- Treat each player as an individual, keeping in mind the wide range of physical and emotional development within the same age group.
- Treat all children equally with respect to gender, race, religion, culture, and ability.
- Be a positive role model by maintaining an attitude of respect, loyalty, patience, courtesy, tact, and maturity.
- Place the emotional and physical well-being of my players ahead of any personal or parental desires to win.
- Lead by example, demonstrating fair play and sportsmanship in my on- and off- field actions.

- Help reinforce the mission and core values (caring, honesty, respect, and responsibility) through my coaching and interactions with others.
- Ensure my team recites the Sports Pledge before each game and shake hands with the opposing team after each game.
- Use coaching techniques that are appropriate for all the ages and skill levels.
- Seek and encourage parental participation at practices, games, and any other activities.
- Respectfully control the behavior of players and parents by asking them to leave the field or sidelines should they become unruly or create an atmosphere that is not appropriate for the development of good sportsmanship.
- Ensure that behavior issues and/or disputes are handled calmly.
- I will encourage the use of and honor the 48-hour calming down period.
- Refrain from the use of tobacco, alcohol, and drugs at all youth sports practices, games, and other events and I will remind others to do the same.
- As a coach, know, abide share, and monitor others for compliance of Child Abuse Prevention standards.
- Utilize positive guidance techniques.
- Refrain from profanity, inappropriate jokes, and sharing of intimate details of my personnel life.
- Exercise good judgment when posting comments on any social media platform regarding players, other coaches, institutions, or athletic officials.
- Own and repair any mistakes made online. Do this in a new post; do not just correct the old post.

I WILL NOT:
- Subject any child to neglect or to mental, verbal, physical, or sexual abuse.
- Leave any child unsupervised.
- Be alone with any child where we cannot be observed by others.
- Transport any children in my vehicle (unless my own child is involved in a neighborhood carpool).
- Attempt to contact or foster a relationship outside of the sports program with any child.

- Give any child gifts or special favors.
- Hold extra or special practices that are not sanctioned by my organization.

The above code of conduct has been established for the safety and well-being of each participant. Failure to adhere to this code of conduct could result in termination of program privileges at all branches.

Parent Tip 22

Every organization must have a Coach's Code of Conduct to protect the players, coaches, and organization. Insist coaches show good sportsmanship when winning and losing.

Parent Tip 23

Organizations and schools must develop a zero tolerance with the coach's code of conduct. Any appearance of inappropriate behavior should be investigated.

Parent Tip 24

Every organization must have training programs for coaches to ensure they are educated on the Coach's Code of Conduct in areas such as: touch, communication (internet, phone, Instagram, Messenger, all aspects and platforms of social media etc.) or sexual misconduct.

1 *Thessalonians* 5:11 "Encourage one another and build one another up. Just as you are doing." *ESV*

Pro-tip From Coach Rome

Sometimes in athletics you win on the scoreboard but you lose the overall game.

Coaches remember the player's attitude reflects your leadership. Teams quite often take on the personality of the coach. Teach determination + dedication = faithfulness and you will be successful in shaping the lives of your athletes.

9 Social Media for Athletes

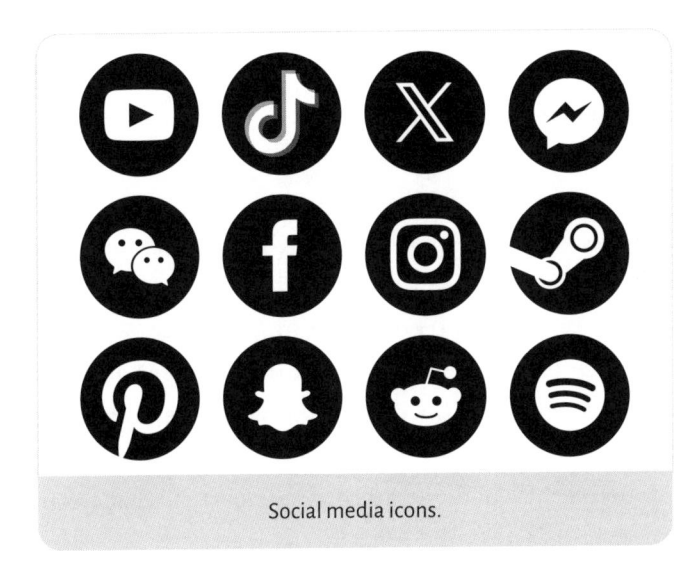

Social media icons.

I attended the University of Dayton School of Law from 2018–2022 obtaining a Master Study of Law and my focus area was social media and cyber law. I have decided to incorporate this aspect of such a prevalent part of life and athletics today in the book. I hope this last chapter is helpful in navigating what is appropriate social media contact for your athlete. Black's Law dictionary defines social media as "Any cell phone or internet-based tools and applications that are used to share and distribute information."[43] The social in social media is the ability for communities to be formed and individuals to exchange content around the information that is posted.[44] Social Media is any technology that allows online conversation.[45] Merriam Webster offers another definition of social media that forms communication (such as websites for social networking and microblogging) through which users create online communities to share information, ideas, personal messages and other content (such as videos). When Kevin was being recruited during his high school football career, social media was not a factor like it is today. I remember when Kevin came to us and wanted to open a MySpace page. Today, coaching my U10 athletes I noticed most of them have cell phones and a few times in the winter 2024, I had to set a rule that there are no phones during practice or games. I have had several players posting shots, plays, and videos on social media such as Tik-Tok. I am not sure why this is relevant for a ten-year-old, but the athletes find value in posting and parents are on board with it. I am not against social media in the life of an athlete if proper boundaries are set for usage. Lawmakers across the country are beginning to agree with this view.

Social media can be a useful tool for development and distraction, but it can be a weapon of mental and athletic destruction in similar ways.[46] Having content go viral can be a thrilling experience for an individual or brand.[47] I wonder if we count the cost of what we are giving up with these posts access and privacy.

One of my favorite scriptures in Luke 14:28 reminds us, "Suppose one of you wants to build a tower. Won't you first sit down and estimate the cost to see if you have enough money to complete it?" NIV

🏷️ Likes in the Life of Athletes Today

Counting the costs might be one of the answers for parents and young athletes when it comes to social media postings. I have seen an athlete have a great game where they were faithful in everything I asked them to do, and we won the game. To my amazement someone in the athlete's family was video-taping certain plays and putting together a video that was posted on Instagram. The athlete was devastated after he got comments like "that wasn't so good," "I have seen better plays," "you did not break any ankles." So, this video did not get very many "Likes" and the athlete wanted to quit playing basketball because he did not get enough "Likes." In my Social Media Law course at the UD School of Law we talked quite extensively about the hidden dangers of the "Like."

"Likes" on social media are a form of communication allowing us to signal our validation and approval with a single click, without having to type anything.[48] "Likes" were first introduced in 2005 by the video site Vimeo, but they really came into the wider public view when they were adopted by Facebook in 2009.[49] At first, Mark Zuckerberg wasn't keen on the idea, but eventually caved to pressure from his team, who were excited about the initial 'Awesome button'.[50] Their reasoning: many posts had a lot of duplicate comments ('Congratulations' 'Well done,' etc.), and a simple "like" button would make it easier for users to signal approval and reduce duplicate comments.[51]

Research I performed in other law classes on suicide prevention and social media has proven that the "Like" has become extremely negative for social media platform users and in some cases has led to suicide. For example, Christine McComas, a fifteen-years-old, took her own life on Easter Sunday in 2012, after a lengthy cyberbullying campaign. After Christine was sexually assaulted, she was further victimized by a cyberbullying campaign alleging she had told on those responsible. The lack of support and "Likes" clearly took a toll on Christine and she took her own life. Since it was popularized by Facebook, "Likes" have become a digital commodity that many young people go to great extents to seek out. Sometimes with negative consequences. I get that impression based on the quote above on the initial reason Facebook launched the like. Not only is the sender inappropriately using the "Like," but it is also being used inappropriately by many receivers. Much more thought needs to go into pressing the "Like" or "Loved It" button. I wonder when I send out important texts to parents if they are even reading the texts because they only respond with

"Like" or "Loved It." A lot of these responses are from people who do not even know us, and we are allowing our mental health to be impacted by their impression or the "Like." There's another, less appreciated, but worrying aspect to "Likes:" Validation, addiction, and how it can affect mental health.[52] Suicide in collegiate sports continues to be an issue. At least five college athletes have died by suicide in recent months, sparking calls for support from the NCAA.[53] Many athletes take to social media to air their feelings and emotions which is not the right venue for emotional support.

Athletes Suffering from Loneliness and Fear of Missing Out

Why are "Likes" so important for athletes who have the world at their feet? One reason might be athletes suffering from loneliness and fear of missing out. Many college athletes think they will be ok until they actually enter college and begin to struggle—it can be hard to find time to balance school, sports, and a social life.[54] Athletes may reject all the wonderful programs available on campus such as teambuilding at university centers or clubs connecting with new teammates and classmates may not be appealing especially when there is simply not enough time. As a result, athletes may find themselves lured by the convenience of social media. If the athlete is not careful, they may find themselves the victim of a nasty social media controversy. This is what happened to Manti Te'o, Notre Dame linebacker and runner up to the 2012 Heisman Trophy. Turns out Te'o was a victim of catfishing, and the woman was not real. Given Te'o's national prominence because he was such a popular college athlete, this whole scandal played out in the media. I am a Notre Dame fan and have been since I was a young boy. This situation with Te'o broke my heart but is an example of how social media can ruin an athlete's life if they are not careful. Te'o had everything going his way, but I believe the demands on him athletically along with his loneliness drove him to take unnecessary risks on social media and now his name will be forever remembered more for this scandal verses being a wonderful football player. Loneliness with athletes has even led to suicide.

Athletes are spending far too much time on social media instead of working on their game and academics. Data shows that 97% of teens are now online daily, up from 92% in 2014–15.[55] We looked at a few athletes' screen time with their permission.[56] When asked what they do for fun, the typical response was, "I get on my phone."[57] Many athletes are so tuned into their phones because they fear if they put it down even for a minute they may miss something important. Fear of Missing Out refers to the feeling or perception that others are having more fun, living better lives, or experiencing better things than you are as an athlete. Commitment to college athletics has been likened to having a full-time job. Balance is key in the life of the athlete if they are going to successfully engage in the full college experience. Zack Harper offers the following tips in his article "Understanding Fear of Missing Out (FOMO) and its Impact on Student Athletes:"

1. Set boundaries for social media use and allocate specific times for engagement.
2. Practice mindfulness and be fully present in the current moment.
3. Focus on your personal achievements and celebrate your own successes.
4. Build a support network of friends, coaches, and mentors who understand the unique challenges faced by student-athletes.
5. Seek professional help if you find that anxiety symptoms persist or significantly impact your daily life.

When an athlete is in elementary, middle, and high school, parents bear responsibility for managing the athlete's social media usage. Some high school athletic departments have rules on social media athletic postings. Colleges and universities have their own separate social media policies for athletes. These institutions have compliance departments to help monitor what the athletes post. The smart play here is to minimize what an athlete posts and stay away from hot topics such as coaches, teams and personal stories that are private. Parents and athletes should familiarize themselves with this set of helpful guidelines from the NCAA and prospective colleges. Athletes should also know that social media works both ways and colleges will check out their social media pages in the recruiting process. The University of Florida withdrew a scholarship offer for Nease High School quarterback Marcus Stokes after video of him rapping along to a song using a racial slur surfaced on social media.[58]

A trash-talking, profane tweet cost a New Hampshire boys basketball player his state Player of the Year award.[59] A Division I college program in North Carolina stopped recruiting a quarterback because its recruiting coordinator thought it excessive for a player to post sixteen times a day on social media.[60] An Ohio soccer player was suspended from his team after he retweeted a picture of a lighter and what appeared to be pot with the message, *"Marijuana is my favorite."*[61]

We must work harder to educate our athletes about the issue of privacy and the rules of social media. In a perfect world we could tell our athletes to stay off social media because it may do more harm than good. Nothing is private!!! We must encourage our athletes to combat loneliness and fear of missing out with other avenues than social media on campus such as clubs, organizations, student groups, friendships etc.

Students: Dos and Don'ts for Social Media Usage

Andrea Gribble, a parent and former schoolteacher in Minnesota, launched *#SocialSchool4EDU* in 2014 to help schools create and use their own social media channels.[62] The bullet points below are from Andrea Gribble.

- *Do:* Praise teammates and team efforts.
- *Don't:* Bash opposing teams or individual players.
- *Do:* Thank fans for their support.
- *Don't:* Swear or misspell words.
- *Do:* Realize you are a role model for many younger students at your school.
- *Don't:* Harass others or mention race, religion, sexual orientation, or physical conditions.
- *Do:* Know that if you retweet or share something, you own it!

Freedom of Speech Challenges

Concluding this chapter, I would like to talk about some freedom of speech challenges that I continue to hear about regarding social media usage. Many athletes have been social influencers in the past and for sure in the modern day. The difference with past collegiate athletes and today's athletes is the use of social media adding to many male and female college athlete's influencer status. With all the content and conversations that the social media explosion has enabled, numerous legal concerns have risen around the creation, posting, and sharing of content.[63] One example today is the rise of sports gambling in college athletics and the dangers sports gambling has placed on athletes through social media. The NCAA has taken notice of the challenges that sports gambling and social media are creating for athletes. The growing abuse athletes, coaches and officials face on social media related to betting has put the NCAA on high alert, an issue addressed this week during the organization's convention in Phoenix.[64] Even though bettors cannot place bets on a player's individual performance in college sports, athletes are still subject to hate and abuse online after a game.[65] This has been heightened over the last few years, as the new generation of bettors and college athletes have grown up around social media and are more likely to post and check their desired platforms.[66]

Professional sports are at a different level where the athletes face other challenges. I see in professional football, for example, family members tweet information about their athlete such as they want to be traded. Information is constantly being leaked regarding athlete contracts on social media. In the summer of 2023, we saw constant leaks about the contracts of football quarterbacks Lamar Jackson of the Baltimore Ravens and Joe Burrow of the Cincinnati Bengals. Yes, these athletes and their family members are perfectly within their legal rights, as expressed in the First Amendment of the Constitution, to express their opinions but with these social media posts they are shooting themselves in the foot. Some of the information leaks come from their family members or own camps and may hurt the athlete in good faith contractual negotiations.

The second part of the First Amendment I hear argued today regarding freedom of speech on social media. Submitting a comment on a social media post is easier to classify as speech, but the issue of whether a simple interaction, such as a "Like" on Facebook could be considered speech was an open question in the early days of social media."[67] I talked earlier about athletes glamorizing the "Like" on social media. I want to point out the serious nature of using terms on social media that are "fluid" or they mean different things. Just because we have the freedom to express ourselves does not mean we always should. Weighing the costs vs. benefits for athletes must be taken more seriously to understand the consequences of overusage.

The bottom line for all of us as parents is we must be careful when allowing our athletes to use social media. We must do more to protect our young children under thirteen and ensure the Children's Online Privacy Protection Act (COPPA) is being followed. COPPA was created to make sure website providers are adhering to privacy laws that require verifiable consent from a parent or guardian for a child to access sites. Although legislation has been slow, states such as Ohio and Arkansas are beginning to enact social media legislation to further protect our children which in turn should help young athletes. Florida Gov. Ron DeSantis (R) signed strong restrictions against children using social media, following other Republican-led states amid a national push to crack down on minors' access to online platforms over safety fears.[68] The sweeping restrictions prohibit children thirteen and younger from creating social media profiles, and requires parental consent for those between fourteen and fifteen.[69] Under the new law, social media platforms will be required to delete existing accounts for children younger than fourteen—though account holders will have a 90-day period to dispute terminations.[70] New York State passed a bill that will restrict the use of algorithms on minors social media feeds, in hopes of addressing mental health concerns.[71]

In December, more than 200 organizations sent a letter urging Senate Majority Leader Chuck Schumer, D-N.Y., to schedule a vote on the Kids Online Safety Act, or KOSA, which seeks to create liability, or a "duty of care," for apps and online platforms that recommend content to minors that can negatively affect their mental health.[72] Social media is a wonderful useful tool to help us communicate whether it be for personal or private usage. Please, be careful and understand the limits of privacy on some platforms. When you decide to allow your athlete to go on platforms such as Tik-Tok, Facebook, Twitter or Instagram please read the fine print. Hopefully, these laws will be passed, and we will have better protection, safety, and security for our athletes. Encourage your athlete not to get involved in rhetoric that may damage their reputation or brand. In a perfect world I would say encourage your athlete to have a plan for social media usage. Understand the high school athletics department policies for the school athletes regarding social media usage.

ENCOURAGE ATHLETES TO PUT DOWN THE CELL PHONE

Athletes, put down your cell phones.

If your high school athlete is being recruited by a college program, familiarize yourself with the NCAA's social media policies. Be aware that for admissions purposes, colleges may look at an athlete's social media page. Athletic compliance departments may also look at an athlete's social media page and posts. A great rule for the athletes is if it does not feel right then do not post it. If a message is prepared and it seems explosive, please think long and hard before pressing send. Families should have a social media plan for their athletes. Limited data show that social media use by athletes affects body image, stress levels, sleep quality and athletic performance.[73] These apps can also foster engagement and connection, secure financial support, and build team cohesion; thus, social media use must be viewed on a continuum.[74] Social media training would likely benefit athletes at all levels.[75] A final thought we most often forget is that there is no permanent delete button on social media and what is posted can undermine a high school, collegiate and professional athletes reputation, quality of life and professional career. I am a fan of social media and realize the complexity of its use today, but I also believe "If assigned the holy task of editing the Bible, social media would be added as the Eighth Plague of Revelation."[76]

Social Media Tips for Athletes to Avoid Common Pitfalls

- Demonstrate good sportsmanship by example and encourage it from fellow players.
- Play the game by the rules.
- View playing athletics as an opportunity to be faithful, learn and have fun.
- Remain respectful toward other players, coaches, referees, and spectators by not posting personal comments or photos offensive to all parties stated.
- Never argue or complain about sporting officials, calls or decisions, especially through social media.
- Make every effort to attend *all* practices and games and arrive on time.
- Be faithful with your academics, treasuring the opportunity to learn and grow in the classroom.
- Never use foul language during games, practice or on social media.
- Be smart about what you publish. When in doubt consult your athletic department compliance office or social media expert on campus.
- Use good judgment when posting comments on any social media platform when talking about other players, coaches, teams, officials, athletic officials, and institutions. Avoid seeking "Likes."

Parent Tip 25

Parents should train their athletes in the Dos and Don'ts of social media usage and the fear of missing out. Parents should monitor the postings and be connected to their athlete's platforms to have a check and balance. Parents should discourage casual social media usage. Once the athlete is playing for a college or university, the athletic college compliance department may take over monitoring the athletes' postings.

Parent Tip 25 (a)

The social media tips should be a personal contract the athlete has with themselves.

Proverbs 22:6 "Train up a child in the way he should go; even when he is old, he will not depart from it." *ESV*

Pro-tip From Coach Rome

My great-grandmother Momma Rose would always tell me, "Wendell if you don't have nothing good to say keep your mouth shut."

Athletes just because you can post something does not mean you should. Please, consider the consequences before you press the send button. Remember, deleting a post does not mean it is not still out there in cyberspace. Sometimes what you post can be a curse.

In Closing

I began drafting this book in 2011 and it has taken me thirteen years to find the time and courage to complete this project. I have met many youth coaches that got into coaching for all the wrong reasons. Most youth coaches have a child that plays on the team. This is not bad, but a coach must feel called to a life of service and be committed to all the athletes. This is one reason we have such a shortage of coaches today. The second reason might be hesitancy in dealing with off-the-hook parents. I believe if everyone would adopt this philosophy of Winning Is the Result of Faithfulness, then our focus could be on the athlete enjoying their sports without any undue pressures.

Our society is changing, especially with the vast world of social media and social platforms. One thing that has not changed is the psychology of sports and the attachment to the mind of faithfulness. To understand "faithfulness" one must understand the mind. The mind is an embodied and relational process that regulates the flow of energy and information.[77] Faithfulness is a mental and spiritual philosophy of internal connection.

This book is intended to be a resource guide for parents to support their children in athletics at any level. For this book to make sense, parents need to ask the right question. You ask a great question, then you seek out a great answer.[78] The best question that parents need to ask is what is my purpose for allowing my children to participate in athletics? My argument is that every parent should want their child to learn the concept, Winning Is the Result of Faithfulness. The lesson of faithfulness will carry them far beyond their athletic careers. Remember the formula Determination + Dedication = Faithfulness in Athletics. Peace, love, unity, and respect to you all.

Endnotes

1. "The Long Journey Home. Understanding and Ministering to the Sexually Abused." Andrew Schmutzer. 2011. Resource Publications.
2. "No Simple Solution for why Student Athletes Continue to Struggle in the Classroom." College AD. April 24, 2015.
3. Barber, Barrie. *Dayton Daily News*. August 3, 2015, p.1.
4. https://quotefancy.com, last visited March 24, 2024.
5. "Sports Coaching, The Definition Guide." Sai Blackburn. June 25, 2023.
6. "More Americans Support Prayer at Public School Sporting Events Than Taking a Knee for National Anthem." Ian M. Giotti. Christian Post. October 7, 2022.
7. "Coach Mike Krzyzewski: Hoops and Faith" John Hanretty. Relevant Radio. March 28, 2023.
8. "The Four Biggest Problems in Youth Sports Today." John O' Sullivan. Family Values, Problems in Youth Sports Specialization. April 3, 2015.
9. "Twenty-One Reasons College Athletes Get Cut or Quit." Grant Osborne. "Be Successful. Don't Give Up!" April 21, 2022.
10. Ibid.p.1.
11. *Moving Beyond Loss. Real Answers to Real Questions From Real People.* Russell Friedman and John W. James. Taylor Trade Publishing. 2013.
12. "St. Louis Football Coach Shot During Practice by Parent Upset Over Son's Playing Time." Cydney Henderson. *USA Today*. October 15,2023.
13. Ibid, p.1.
14. "Twenty-One Reasons College Athletes Get Cut or Quit." Grant Osborne. "Be Successful. Don't Give Up!" April 21, 2022.
15. "Twenty-One Reasons College Athletes Get Cut or Quit." Grant Osborne. "Be Successful. Don't Give Up!" April 21, 2022.
16. *Crime Online*. Yvonne Jewkes. Willan Publishing. 2007.
17. "Seven Thoughts on How Grades Affect Scholarships." Bryan Drotar. *The Recruiting Code Makes Recruiting Easy.* March 2020.
18. "Twenty-five Essential Business Travel Statistics (2023): How Much do Companies Spend on Business Travel?" Jack Flynn. Business Travel FAQ. March 29, 2023.

[19] Ibid, p.2.
[20] "Mommy Points: The Balancing Act of Work Travel as a Parent." Summer Hull. The Points Guy. April 19, 2019.
[21] Ibid, p.1.
[22] "Should I Get to All My Child's Games?" Tara Parker-Pope. *The New York Times*. June 3, 2010.
[23] "Twenty-One Reasons College Athletes Get Cut or Quit." Grant Osborne. "Be Successful. Don't Give Up!" April 21, 2022.
[24] *The Man in the Mirror, Solving the Twenty-Four Problems Men Face.* Patrick M. Morley. Zondervan Press. 2014.
[25] Ibid, p.1.
[26] "Winning Isn't Everything." Michael W. Austin, PHD. *Psychology Today*. June 12, 2010.
[27] Ibid, p.1.
[28] *The One Thing.* Gary Keller and Jay Papasan. Bard Press. 2012.
[29] "What is Success in Youth Sports?" Sports Parenting. The Jersey Watch Team. Last visited November 20, 2023.
[30] "Maintaining a 'Winning' Focus is Not the Way to Win. There's a Paradox at the Heart of Winning." Warrick Wood, PHD. *Psychology Today*. July 11, 2014.
[31] "What is Success in Youth Sports?" Sports Parenting. The Jersey Watch. Last visited November 20, 2023.
[32] "How to Create a Code of Conduct for Youth Sports." Youth Sports Management. Connie Harrington.
[33] "I'm Just a Kid Who Did Something Wrong." Jere Longman." *The New York Times*. July 16, 2021.
[34] "Fight: Mars Fairmont-Trotwood Girls Basketball Game." Mike Hartsock. December 21, 2017. WHIOTV7.
[35] Ibid, p.1.
[36] Ibid, p.1.
[37] "Ex-Coach Convicted on Sex Charges Now Faces Arson Trial." Nancy Bowman. *Springfield News-Sun*. September 1, 2009.
[38] "Toughen Up Snowflake! Sports Coaches Can be Emotionally Abusive—Here's How to Recognize It." *The Conversation*. Beth Daily. February 24, 2019.
[39] Ibid, p.1.
[40] Ibid, p.1.
[41] Ibid, p.1.
[42] Ibid, p.1.
[43] *Social Media in a Nutshell.* Ryan Garcia and Thaddeus Hoffmeister. West Academic Publishing. 2017.

44 Ibid, p.2.
45 Ibid, p.3.
46 "The Impact of Social Media on Youth Athletes." Luke Smith. Health, Training, Youth Athletes. February 13, 2021.
47 *Social Media in a Nutshell.* Ryan Garcia and Thaddeus Hoffmeister. West Academic Publishing 2017.
48 "The Power of Likes on Social Media: Friend or Foe?" Branwell Moffat. The Future of Commerce. Last visited November 27, 2023.
49 Ibid, p.1.
50 Ibid, p.1.
51 Ibid, p.1.
52 Ibid, p.1.
53 "Reeling From Suicides, College Athletes Press NCAA: This is a Crisis." Molly Hensley-Clancy. *The Washington Post.* May 19, 2022.
54 "Lonely? Three Tips to Help Busy College Athletes Make Friends." Claire Borman. 2aDays. June 27, 2023.
55 "Teenage Social Media Usage Statistics in 2023." Susan Laborde. Tech Report, October 13, 2023.
56 "The Impact of Social Media on Athletes." Luke Smith. The STACK. February 13, 2021.
57 Ibid, p.1.
58 "University of Florida Revokes Football Scholarship After Video Surfaces." TreVaughn Howard www.cbsnews.com. November 21, 2022.
59 "Don't Let One Bad Tweet Ruin an Athlete's Future." Jeff Di Veronica. Democrat and Chronicle. September 6, 2017.
60 Ibid, p.1.
61 Ibid, p.1.
62 Ibid, p.1.
63 *Social Media in a Nutshell.* Ryan Garcia and Thaddeus Hoffmeister. West Academic Publishing. 2017.
64 "NCAA President: College Athletes Face Harassment on Social Media Because of Sports Betting." Jesse Brawders. Cronkite News. January 13, 2024.
65 Ibid, p.1.
66 Ibid, p.1.
67 *Social Media in a Nutshell.* Ryan Garcia and Thaddeus Hoffmeister. West Academic Publishing. 2017.
68 "Florida Latest to Restrict Social Media for Kids as Legal Battle Looms." Maria Luisa Paul, Cristiano Lima-Strong, *Washington Post.* March 25, 2024.
69 Ibid, p.1.

70. Ibid, p.1.
71. "What to Know About New Social Media Protections for Children in New York." Fahy, Claire. *New York Post*. June 13, 2024.
72. Ibid, p.1.
73. "Likes and Hashtags: Influence of Athlete Social Media Use." Sarah Merrill and Marcia Faustin. November 17, 2023. Hogrefe eContent.
74. Ibid, p. 1.
75. Ibid, p.1.
76. "When Social Media is Toxic for Young Athletes." David Udelf Psy.D. *Psychology Today*. December 3, 2023.
77. "The Developing Mind. How Relationships and the Brain Interact to Shape Who We Are." Daniel J. Siegel. The Guilford Press. 2020.
78. *The One Thing, The Surprisingly Simple Truth Behind Extraordinary Results.* Gary Keller with Jay Papasan. Bard Press. 2012.

Bibliography

Making your Marriage Deployment Ready. Mike and Linda Montgomery, Keith, and Sharon Morgan. Family Publishing. Arkansas 2012.

The Five Dysfunctions of a Team. Patrick Lencioni and Josey Bass. California. 2002.

Basketball Skills and Drills. Jerry V. Kraus, Don Meyer, Jerry Meyer. Illinois. 1991.

Difficult Conversations. How to Discuss What Matters Most. Douglas Stone, Bruce Patton, Sheila Heen. Penguin Group. New York. 1999.

Pastoral Care with Stepfamilies. Mapping the Wilderness. Loren L. Townsend. Chalice Press. Missouri 2000.

Saving your Second Marriage Before It Starts. Drs Les and Leslie Parrot. Zondervan. Michigan. 2001.

Bringing up Boys. Dr. James Dobson. Tyndale House Publishers. Illinois. 2001.

7 Habits of Highly Effective Families for Army Families. Dr. John Covey. Franklin Covey Co. 2005.

Faithfulness is Winning in the Kingdom of God. Dave Ferguson and Warren Bird. April 12, 2018. Last Visited October 31, 2023.

Youth Football team suspended after parent allegedly shoots coach in front of kids. *Associated Press.* October 20, 2023. Last visited October 25, 2023.

The One Thing, The Surprisingly Simple Truth Behind Extraordinary Results. Gary Keller with Jay Papasan. Bard Press. 2012.

The Developing Mind: How Relationships and the Brain Interact to Shape Who We Are. Daniel J. Siegel. The Guilford Press. 2020.

Leadership Without Easy Answers. Ronald A. Heifetz. The Belknap Press of Harvard University Press. 1994.

The Man in the Mirror: Solving the 24 Problems Men Face. Patrick M. Morley. Zondervan Press. 2014 latest edition.

Shaping the Man Inside Teenage Boys! Surviving & Enjoying These Extraordinary Years. Bill Beausay. Waterbrook Press. 1996.

The Heart of a Warrior: Before You Can Become the Warrior, You Must Become the Beloved Son. Michael Thompson. Heart and Life Publishers. 2015.

The Purpose Driven Life: What on Earth Am I Here For? Rick Warren. Zondervan Publishing. 2002.

Crime Online. Yvonne Jewkes. Willan Publishing. 2007.

Living in a Stepfamily Without Getting Stepped On: Helping Your Children Survive the Birth Order. Dr. Kevin Leman. Thomas Nelson Publishers. 1994.

Moving Beyond Loss: Real Answers To Real Questions From Real People. Russell Friedman and John W. James. Taylor Trade Publishing. 2013.

The Serving Leader: Five Powerful Actions to Transform Your Team, Business, and Community. Kenneth R. Jennings and John Stahl-Wert. Berrett- Koehler Publishers, Inc. 2016.

Straight A Leadership: Alignment Action Accountability. Quint Studer. Fire Starter Publishing. 2009.

The Long Journey Home: Understanding and Ministering to the Sexually Abused. Andrew Schmutzer. 2011. Resource Publications

Barber, Barrie. *Dayton Daily News.* August 3, 2015. Last visited October 25, 2023.

Child Sexual Abuse Among Boys. Raychelle Cassada, Lohmann. *U.S. News.* November 26, 2018

Sexual Abuse. Reviewed by Psychology today, Staff. *Psychology Today.* Last visited November 17, 2023.

Child Sexual Abuse Statistics. Natasha Tracy. *Healthy Place.* December 30, 2021.

No simple solution for why student athletes continue to struggle in the classroom. *College AD.* April 24, 2015. Last visited September 6, 2022.

Sports Coaching, The definition guide. Sai Blackburn. June 25, 2023. Last visited August 9, 2023.

The 4 Biggest Problems in youth sports today. John O' Sullivan. Family Values, Problems in youth Sports Specialization. April 3, 2015. Last visited October 15, 2023.

2017 U.S. Census Bureau. Same Sex Couple Households.

St. Louis football coach shot during practice by parent upset over son's playing time. Cydney Henderson. *USA today.* October 15,2023. Last visited October 32, 2023.

Essential business travel statistics (2023): How much do companies spend on business travel. Jack Flynn. Business travel FAQ. March 29, 2023. Last visited June 2, 2023.

Mommy Points: The Balancing Act of Work Travel as a Parent. Summer Hull. The Points Guy. April 19, 2019. Last visited November 1, 2023.

Should I Get to All My Child's Games? Tara Parker – Pope. *The New York Times.* June 3, 2010. Last visited December 1, 2023.

Winning Isn't Everything. Michael W. Austin, PHD. *Psychology Today.* June 12, 2010. Last visited December 1, 2023.

The One Thing. Gary Keller and Jay Papasan. Bard Press. 2012.

What is success in youth sports. Sports Parenting. The Jersey Watch Team. Last visited November 20, 2023.

Maintaining a "Winning" Focus is not the way to win. There's a paradox at the heart of winning. Warrick Wood, PHD. *Psychology Today.* July 11, 2014. Last visited June 1, 2023.

What is success in youth sports. Sports Parenting. The Jersey Watch. Last visited November 20, 2023.

With Average NFL career 3.3 years, players motivated to complete MBA program. John Keim. www.espn.com/blog. June 29, 2016. Last visited July 3, 2023.

How to create a code of conduct for youth sports. Youth Sports Management. Connie Harrington. Last visited August 8, 2023.

I'm just a kid who did something wrong. Jere Longman. *The New York Times.* July 16, 2021. Last visited November 3, 2023.

Fight Mars Fairmont-Trotwood girls basketball game. Mike Hartsock. December 21, 2017. WHIOTV7. Last visited November 15, 2023.

Ex-coach convicted on sex charges now faces arson trial. Nancy Bowman. *Springfield News–Sun.* September 1, 2009. Last visited November 14, 2023.

Toughen up snowflake! Sports coaches can be emotionally abusive – here's how to recognize it. The Conversation. Beth Daily. February 24, 2019. Last visited September 30, 2023.

With Average NFL career 3.3 years, players motivated to complete MBA program. John Keim. www.espn.com/blog. June 29, 2016.

Here's what a "Like" really means on every social media platform. Nicholas DiDomzio. www.mic.com. July 8, 2015. Last visited December 3, 2023.

How many smartphones are in the world today. Ash Turner. July 2020. www.bankingcell.com. Last visited December 7, 2023.

More Americans support prayer at public school sporting events than taking a knee for National Anthem. Ian M. Giotti. *Christian Post.* October 7, 2022. Last visited December 15, 2023.

Lonely? 3 Tips to help busy college athletes make friends. Claire Borman. 2aDays. June 27, 2023. Last visited December 11, 2023.

The truth behind the Monti Te'o fake girlfriend saga was even weirder than you thought. Sheila Flynn. *Independent.* August 15, 2022. Last visited December 11, 2023.

Here's how social media is causing a negative impact on athletes and sports. Gurpartap Mann. March 8, 2023. LinkedIn. Last visited December 16, 2023.

When social media is toxic for young athletes. David Udelf Psy.D. *Psychology Today.* December 3, 2023. Last visited December 16, 2023.

Hogrefe eContent. November 17, 2023. Last visited December 16, 2023.

Coach Mike Krzyzewski: Hoops and Faith. John Hanretty. Relevant Radio. March 28, 2023.

21 Reasons College Athletes Get Cut or Quit. Grant Osborne. Be Successful. Don't Give Up! April 22, 2022.

NCAA President: College athletes face harassment on social media because of sports betting. Jesse Brawders. *Cronkite News.* January 13, 2024.

Sports parents are out of control and officials don't feel safe. Here's what's at risk. Stephen Borelli. *USA today.* October 15, 2023.

Understanding Fear of Missing Out (FOMO) and its impact on Student Athletes. Zack Harper. *NIL TasteMaker Insider.* June 24, 2023.

Florida latest to restrict social media for kids as legal battle looms. Maria Luisa Paul, Cristiano Lima-Strong. *Washington Post.* March 25, 2024.

7 Thoughts on Grades Affect Athletic Scholarships. Bryan Drotar. The Recruiting Code Makes Recruiting Easy. March 2020.

What to Know About New Social Media Protections for Children in New York. Fahy, Claire. *New York Post.* June 13, 2024. Last visited June 14, 2024.

About the Author

Lieutenant Colonel Wendell K. Rome served in the United States Air Force for thirty-five years before retiring on May 8, 2016, as the Wing Chaplain at the 132 FW Des Moines, Iowa. Chaplain Rome also served as the Chief of Chaplain Service and Senior Pastor of the historic Home Protestant Church at the Dayton Veterans Administration before retiring in March of 2022. He has been a member of Kappa Alpha Psi Incorporated since spring 1994. Dr. Rome received his Doctor of Ministry (2003) and Master of Divinity (2001) from United Theological Seminary in Dayton, Ohio. He received his master's in public policy (1994) from the University of Northern Iowa and Master Study of Law from the University of Dayton School of Law

(2022). He is a proud graduate of Southern University in New Orleans where he received his BS in Business (1990). Coach Rome has served as a coach collaborating with both boys and girls for thirty-three years. His coaching experience includes soccer, wrestling, baseball, basketball, and girls volleyball. He served seven years as the football team Chaplain at Dayton Christian School in Dayton, Ohio. He has coached both boys and girls from ages 4-19. Today, he coaches a 12U basketball team at the Kleptz YMCA in Englewood, Ohio. He is currently a teaching associate in the Boonshoft Wright State University School of Medicine and is the proud owner of WKKDRRL Social Media and Cyber Law consulting company. He is married to Kathleen and together they have raised seven children.

Coach Rome's Coaching Record

Football .... 60 games football team chaplain
Basketball 181-94
Soccer 55-11
Volleyball 5-4
Wrestling 5-1
Total Record 291-145
Total games coached 436
Winning percentage 68%

Note: Games as varsity assistant coach not included

Twenty-five Parent Tips
(A Summary)

Parent Tip 1
Do not use academics as a tool for discipline. Instead set academic goals that are realistic for your athlete and well communicated between player and coach.

Parent Tip 2
Do ask the coach for a mid-term and final season player evaluation on your athlete.

Parent Tip 3
Do encourage the importance of faith in the life of your athlete.

Parent Tip 4
Do not be an off-the-hook parent. Respect your athlete, the coach, and organization your athlete competes with.

Parent Tip 5
Do impart positive energy to your athlete. This is not about you!

Parent Tip 6
Do remember what God has called you to do in the life of your athlete. Be encouraging, positive, and supportive of their coaching staff and the organization of participation.

Parent Tip 7
Do not force your athlete to play a sport that they do not want to play.

Parent Tip 8

Do be realistic about what your athlete's gifts and talents are athletically and academically.

Parent Tip 9

Do involve other family members, parents, if possible, to support the athlete. For example, divorced families can work together. Communication between families is the key.

Parent Tip 10

If your athlete has a disability such as ADD, ADHD or any other medical diagnosis, do get together with the coaching staff immediately and let them know what the athlete is dealing with so adjustments can be made for the player if needed.

Parent Tip 11

Do not be afraid to discuss your unique family system with the coaching staff, administration etc.

Parent Tip 12

Parents should be familiar with the institution's Athletic Handbook on policies and procedures, especially the playing time or participation policy.

Parent Tip 13

Parents should build a positive relationship with their athletes' coaches, athletic director, and school officials.

Parent Tip 14

Do develop an action plan in the athlete's sophomore year of high school to include goals for academics and athletics. This should include the athlete, coaching staff, parents, and athlete's academic advisor/counselor. Track the plan and provide updates to the coaching staff. Do not be afraid to reach out to college coaches during that sophomore year.

Parent Tip 15
Do use social media as a positive tool to get exposure for your athlete to prospective colleges. Send game films and high school transcripts to the college's athletic website. Always post the best two or three game plays of the week. Do not seek "Likes." This is strictly for prospective colleges or universities.

Parent Tip 16
Do communicate with your athlete as much as possible while you are away from home. Be open and honest about your travel commitments. Communicate your schedule with the athlete and develop an action plan for support.

Parent Tip 17
When reintegrating back home from deployment or long business trip do have a reintegration plan in supporting your athlete.

Parent Tip 18
One thing in the life of athletics that parents must teach their athletes is to be faithful, win or lose. In other words, learning how to lose is critical and all about attitude. Losing can be a blessing. It encourages opportunity for growth and further development in being faithful.

Parent Tip 19
Parents should ensure that their athletes never believe that winning at all costs is more important than academics or citizenship.

Parent Tip 20
Parents should not be encouraged to post fights and disruptive player behavior on social media. There is no value to the athlete in doing so.

Parent Tip 21

Organizations must adopt a zero tolerance with parents who choose not to follow the Code of Conduct. Ensure the Code is communicated and signed by the parent or guardian. Enforcing compliance is the key.

Parent Tip 22

Every organization must have a Coach's Code of Conduct to protect the players, coaches, and organization. Enforcing compliance for organizations is the key. Coaches must comply with the organization's social media policies also.

Parent Tip 23

Organizations and schools must develop a zero tolerance policy with the coaches. The appearance of inappropriate behavior should be investigated and addressed immediately.

Parent Tip 24

Every organization must have training programs for coaches to ensure they are educated on the Coach's Code of Conduct in areas such as: appropriate touch, alone time with athletes, outside communication (social media, internet, phone, Instagram, Messenger etc.) or sexual misconduct.

Parent Tip 25

Parents should train their athletes on the Dos and Don'ts of social media usage. Parents, familiarize yourselves with the ever changing youth social media laws statewide and nationally.

Parent Tip 25(a)

Player social media tips should be a personal contract the athlete has with themselves.

Sample Practice Plan 12U

Determination + Dedication = Faithfulness
Focus on lay-ups and free throws
Irish (Team Name)
Coach Rome   Practice 2   6/17/24.

6:55-7:00	Stretch, Introductions
7:00-7:10	Lay-ups at all three baskets (reverse/rebound/putback)
7:10-7:15	Suicide dribbling; four corner dribbling
7:15-7:20	1-2-2, 1-3-1, and 3-2 defense
7:20-7:25	Rebounding into outlet passes
7:25-7:30	4 low offensive set
7:30-7:35	Water break (Around the world shooting), focus shot selection (layups and free throws focus)
7:35-7:40	Sprints into free throws
7:40-7:45	4 low offensive set
7:45-7:50	Defensive stance, shuffle feet
7:50-7:55	Scrimmage
8:00	Pre-game talk (bedtime, heavy meal breakfast, report time 2:30pm, location game Kleptz)

Sample Practice Plan Junior High Basketball

Determination + Dedication = Faithfulness

Bulls (Team Name)

Coach Rome   Practice 6   2/22/24

7:00-7:05	Stretching
7:05-7:10	On the wall rebounding: Focus, rebounding technique boxing out.
7:10-7:15	Suicide dribbling
7:15-7:20	Layups all three rims: Focus, dribbling, conditioning, rebounding, finishing at the rim.
7:20-7:30	4-low offensive set: Focus, positioning, ball movement, talking, shot selection.
7:30-7:32	2-3 defensive set: Focus, talking, spacing, recovering, active hands.
7:32-7:40	Suicides into free throws: focus conditioning, making free throws while winded.
7:40-7:45	Stack under basket: focus positioning, shot selection, ball movement.
7:45-7:50	Man-to-man defensive set: focus on talking, active hands, finding your man, recovering, rebounding, outlet passes.
7:50-7:55	Press breaker: focus, getting the ball up the court by passing, spacing, good quality shots, situational basketball, taking care of the ball.
8:00	Closing Points: Where we play, what time, opponent (brief game plan).

Sample Letters for Parents to Recruiting College Coaches

🐚 Sample Letter Between Wendell Rome and Coach of Ohio Dominican College

Date: Thursday, October 23, 2008, 6:32 AM
From: Dr. Wendell Rome
To: Chris Oliver
Subject: Kevin Washington (Ohio Dominican)

Reginald Kevin Washington
Senior wide receiver Dayton Christian High School

Greetings from Balad AFB, Iraq. I am Dr. Wendell K. Rome and we spoke through email last year about my son Reginald Kevin Washington a senior wide receiver from Dayton Christian High School in Dayton, Ohio. Kevin is represented by NCSA (National Collegiate Scouting Association) which is where you saw his game film.

I wanted you to know that Kevin has applied to Ohio Dominican and been accepted. We would now like to discuss the possibilities of him playing football at ODU. Our home phone number is 937- 854-0487. I will be returning to the states in January, and we would love to come for a visit to check out the campus and meet the coaching staff.

Please, let us know your thoughts. We can also send you a game film. If you desire to see the film from Kevin's senior season, please email a good address and we will get it to you.

Thanks in advance for your time,

Sincerely,

Dr. Rome

Date: Wednesday, October 29, 2008, 6:05
From: Chris Oliver
To: Dr. Wendell Rome
Subject: Kevin Washington (Ohio Dominican)

Dr. Rome,

Please send film to:
Football Office

Thanks.

🏈 Sample Letter Between Wendell Rome and Oberlin University

Date: Sun, Dec 21, 2008, at 6:57 AM
From: Dr. Wendell Rome
To: Kevin Wahl
Subject: Kevin Washington

Season's greetings Coach Wahl,

Can you verify for me if Oberlin has received all of Kevin's application materials? According to the school at Dayton Christian everything has been sent off.

Thanks,
Dr. Rome

Date: Monday, December 22, 2008, 5:30 PM
From: Kevin Wahl
To: Dr. Wendell Rome
Subject: Kevin Washington

Dr. Rome,

Just checked our database, and the last two recommendations have been entered into the system. Our records show that we have received all of Kevin's application materials in full.

Knowing that Kevin's Application is complete is sure a load off my mind, as I'm sure it is for you and Kevin. Thank you for checking with the school.

Have a safe and happy holiday,
Coach Wahl

Coach Rome's Player Evaluation Form

Player Name: _____

Summary: _____

Defense Overall:
Attitude:
Discipline:
Rebounding:
Energy:
Effort:
Taking Plays Off:

Offense Overall:
Shot Selection:
Ball Handling:
Lay-ups:
Jump-shots:
Dribbling:
Turnovers:
Assists:
Free Throws:
Confidence:

Running-The-Floor Overall:
Conditioning:
Running Lanes:
Confidence:
Transition Offense to Defense:
Transition Defense to Offense:

Other Overall:
Teamwork:
Supporting Teammates:
Basketball IQ:
Faithfulness:

Evaluation Key:
1 — Needs Improvement
2 — Minimal Balling
3 — Satisfactory Balling
4 — Excellent Balling
5 — Outstanding Balling